ADD
TO
YOUR
FAITH

ADD TO YOUR FAITH

Biblical Teaching on Christian Maturity

SINCLAIR B. FERGUSON

Pickering & Inglis
LONDON · GLASGOW

ISBN 0 7208 0463 9
Cat. No. 01/0132

First printing 1980

His divine power has given us everything we need for life
and godliness ... For this very reason, make every effort to
add to your faith ...

2 Peter 1:3, 5 (NIV)

Contents

Introduction

The basic theme of the following pages is Christian growth and maturity. It is an important subject and one of vital interest for every Christian. It is not possible however to grow as a Christian simply by reading a book about maturity, any more than it is possible to cultivate a garden by purchasing a gardening manual! For that reason this series of studies offers no short-cuts or instant packages for the Christian life. Instead it offers a series of studies based on various important and relevant passages of the Bible. Each chapter consists of a practical exposition of one or possibly two passages. The method is not accidental for the understanding and application of Scripture is itself one of the ways in which God enables us to grow in grace and the knowledge of Christ. It is really of great importance that our Christian life should be built not on a few texts of the Bible only, nor on some illuminating illustration, or for that matter on the help someone else has discovered in a passage of Scripture, but on our own grasp of those truths in the word of God which will build us up as children of God and strengthen us in our Christian walk.

It will almost certainly increase the value of reading these pages and the benefit of the studies themselves if they are read with a Bible at hand. The version which is used and quoted throughout is mainly the *New International Version*.

No book, long or short, is ever written without its author incurring debts! I am indebted to the many friends in whose lives I have witnessed the outworking in practical terms of the biblical principles this book attempts to expound; to Nicholas Gray of Pickering and Inglis, who first suggested these pages, and has encouraged me during their writing; and chiefly to my wife Dorothy. It is very largely in the years in which I have been the recipient of her love and friendship that God has taught me in some measure the lessons which these studies endeavour to share. It is my own prayer that God may use the chapters which follow to encourage you to 'add to your faith'.

Glasgow   Sinclair B. Ferguson
January 1980

Growing up

1
The importance of maturity

At the heart of the teaching of the New Testament lie a few fundamental, burning concerns.

The chief of these is a desire for the glory of God. The means by which that is to be promoted is the evangelisation of the world. But alongside these twin goals, in the hearts of the writers of the New Testament letters lay a deep-seated concern to promote both the glory of God and the church's impact on the world by the growth and development of every Christian to spiritual maturity.

If that was the concern of the first Christians; if it is one of the burdens of the teaching of the New Testament, should it not inevitably be one of our major concerns also? Yet the bringing of men, women and young people to Christian maturity is a task left largely neglected in the contemporary church. To too many of us Paul's words have a devastating appropriateness: 'Brothers, I could not address you as spiritual but as worldly — mere infants in Christ. I gave you milk, not solid food, for you were not yet ready for it. Indeed, you are still not ready' (1 Cor. 3:1, 2).

I cannot think of the subject of Christian maturity without being reminded of a talk I once heard, given to a group of young people with whom I was involved. The speaker was an American representative of a fairly well-known evangelistic mission. I cannot easily forget how he told us of the decision he made to go to Bible School for a year 'to get maturity'! But true

3

Christian growth and the production of a fully-developed
Christian character expressing itself in consistent Christian
living cannot be quite so easily purchased. It requires patient
building, and it can be gained only in the school of the
Christian life by the pursuit of a course specially geared by
God to the needs, gifts and service of the individual Christian.

HINDRANCES TO MATURITY

It is not easy for many Christians today to devote themselves
to the long term work of God in their lives.

The kind of society we live in militates against maturity. The
consumer-centred,   instant-creation,   media-dominated,
package-deal civilisation of our times is not well suited to the
long process which helps to produce *character*. Nor does it
produce 'characters' —men and women who stand out in
society, who add to its dimensions simply because they are
different by being themselves. On the contrary, our society
abounds in the rather ludicrous spectacle of people determined
to be different by being the replica of others, moulded by the
transient fashions of the moment, whose distinctiveness is a
rather pathetic sameness and unoriginality. It is not easy,
especially for young people in such a pressurised world, to
devote themselves to those influences which will pay
dividends *over the long term*. But if we would be mature we
must renounce our hunger for immediate returns and in that
sense refuse to be squeezed into the mould of our world.

**The background of many Christians militates against
maturity.** That may seem a strange statement. After all, it is
surely not my background which makes me a Christian.
Agreed, but it is largely my background which creates the
basic stuff of my personality, the 'me' that becomes a
Christian, and goes on to live the Christian life. Many people
becoming Christians today have never been exposed to the
kind of influences in life which help to mould and develop
character — and sometimes we may feel as a result that it is

almost impossible to recapture lost ground, or to make up for lost time. If it is true, as one poet liked to think that

> The world is too much with us,
> Getting and spending we lay waste our powers

then the recovery of those devastated powers will not be the task of a single day.

The kind of Christian influences to which we are exposed may not promote maturity. Sadly, that is the conclusion to which many senior Christians are driven as they try to assess the times in which we live. There is abroad a spirit of lament in the hearts of some of the least critical men and women of Christian experience. Two symptoms of a malaise in contemporary Christian living are often underlined as the cause of this concern. *There is so little seriousness* — it is not unknown to witness the message of eternal life being presented today after the audience has been warmed up by preliminaries resembling a pantomime. It is even more extraordinary to discover that this is being done by sincere Christians who believe the Bible to be the word of God, but have never reflected on the way in which the gospel was presented by Christ and his apostles. *There is too little teaching* — the food of God's word which builds Christians up in their faith is sometimes denied them, either because it is wrongly assumed that the only teaching necessary is the basic elements of the gospel and thereafter Christians can be left to their own devices, or because a premium is placed on experience, whether it be our own experience or the biographical experiences of others, rather than on God and his word.

It is more than likely that a reader who selects a book with a title like this will be inclined to agree. You are conscious of a desire to go on in your Christian life, to become a useful, mature, consistent Christian. You are also conscious of these obstacles and others, however unexpressed they are. It need not therefore be a spirit of criticism which makes us recognise the difficulties around us, but a spirit of humble realism. But we have an assurance that all of these difficulties were faced in one form or another by the writers of the pages of Scripture. We face no difficulties which are novel.

In fact, it was to exactly this kind of situation that the Letter to the Hebrews was addressed. The recipients were in great danger of allowing the world to squeeze them into its mould (cf. Rom. 12:1, 2, J. B. Phillips' translation). Persecution was hanging over their heads and some of their number had already suffered for the cause of Christ (Heb. 13:3). Some of them were conscious of a deepening spirit of lethargy setting in. There was danger of *going back*, of *giving up* the race, of *sinking under* the pressures. So the writer of the letter — a 'word of exhortation' as he calls it (13:22) — encourages them with these stirring words:

'*let us ... go on to maturity*' (6:1).

The word which is translated 'mature' in the New Testament is also sometimes translated by the English words 'perfect' or 'complete'. It belongs to a little family of words in the New Testament — a verb, adjective, and noun — which convey the idea of completeness or wholeness.

The word 'mature' could be used to describe a sacrifice which was without blemish, and generally conveyed the idea of completeness — nothing lacking, or left out, or out of place. A *full* year, or a *full* life would be translated partly by this same word, *teleios*. A *full* number for the Greeks was one which was the sum of all the other numbers by which it could be divided — like 6 (the sum of 1, 2, and 3) or 28 (the sum of 1, 2, 4, 7 and 14). It was complete and 'perfect' in itself.

The same word had other interesting uses. It meant to reach a high level of competence — as a doctor, or teacher, or even as a thief! To be perfect in this sense meant to have one's powers and talents fully-developed. Obviously it had no moral content. And, of course, the word meant 'completed', 'finished' in the sense that we might speak of the 'finished article', often meaning not merely that the work had been completed, but that it was an article of quality, created by the considerable skill of some craftsman. Thus, naturally, in ordinary use it came to denote adult behaviour and the opposite of childish play.

These different examples help to illustrate the sense in which the New Testament speaks about Christian maturity.

In general terms the mature Christian is one in whom God's purposes to recreate him have become evident (cf. 2 Cor. 5:17; Eph. 2:10).

James speaks in this way about the trials of Christian experience, which are the chisel marks of the Master Craftsman upon us: 'Perseverance must finish its work so that you may be mature and complete, not lacking anything' (Jas. 1:4). 'Not lacking anything' — a stable, capable Christian whose gifts and graces have been developed so that by God's grace he is master of himself, and able to use all that God has given him in his service. A Christian whose rough edges have been finely planed by the Holy Spirit; one who has been 'filled out' by a character which shows the fruit of the Spirit; someone whose life manifests the qualities which only Jesus Christ can produce. This is maturity.

THE NECESSITY OF MATURITY

Maturity is an essential part of the goal of the Christian's life simply because he is a Christian, and by definition shares in fellowship with Jesus Christ, and hears the call to follow his example. *We must go on to maturity, because Jesus went on to maturity.*

We think of that too infrequently, perhaps because we are always conscious of the need to safeguard our Lord's distinctiveness as the Son of God. But the New Testament teaches with equal emphasis that he was made like us in order to be the Pioneer of salvation (Heb. 2:10) — that is the first one in whom perfect obedience, whole-hearted service, a complete exhibition of the fruit of the Spirit and maturity of character, should be seen. Implied in this statement about Christ is the idea that he now stands before us revealing himself to us, and calling us both to share in what he has done for us by drawing on the resources of his grace, experience and power, and to imitate him in the way he grew into a mature and complete servant of God.

(a) The Example of Jesus
In fact we might go so far as to say that the picture of Christ

B

given to us in the Letter to the Hebrews is a picture of *Christ the Mature*. The 'maturity' family of words appears something like eighteen times in this one letter. We are told that Christ became mature through his sufferings (2:10). That does not mean he improved himself morally. He was always holy and perfect in his obedience to God. What it does mean is that as he grew physically, mentally, and in experience as a man, his obedience and faithfulness to God developed correspondingly, and as his natural capacity grew so he increasingly manifested the fruit of the Spirit. As a boy he was God's boy; as a youth he was God's youth, totally; as a mature man, he maturely demonstrated what God's grace is able to perform in the life which is yielded entirely to him.

This biblical emphasis was given beautiful expression by one of the most important Christian writers of the early church, Irenaeus of Lyons (c. AD 130-200). In his work entitled *Against Heresies* he says this:

> Christ did not reject humanity nor go beyond its limitations; he did not abrogate his laws for the human race in his own case. Instead he sanctified each stage of life ... He came to save all through his own person; all that is, who through him are re-born to God; infants, children, boys, young men and old. Therefore he passed through every stage of life. He was made an infant for infants, sanctifying infancy; a child among children, sanctifying childhood, and setting an example of filial affection, of righteousness and obedience; a young man among young men, becoming an example to them, and sanctifying them to the Lord. So also he was a grown man among the older men, that he might be a perfect teacher for all, not merely in respect of revelation of the truth, but also in respect of this stage of life, sanctifying the older men, and becoming an example to them also. And thus he came even to death, that he might be 'the first-born from the dead, having the pre-eminence among all, or in all things' (Col. 1:18), the author of Life, who goes before all and shows the way.
>
> (II:xxxii, 4)

It is Luke the physician, with his deep interest in all that is connected with human life, who comments that from his early years Jesus grew in stature and wisdom, and correspondingly in favour with God as well as man (Luke 2:42). If that is not part and parcel of our picture of Jesus, then we have not yet really grasped what our Lord's true humanity means. But even when we begin to catch a glimpse of the deep significance of these words there is something mysterious about them. Yes, Jesus developed. *He was never a man disguised as a boy.* For all his serious-minded and sincerely-asked questions as a twelve-year old boy, he was a boy then and not a man. He had to grow. He did not have the wisdom which only divinely-planned experience would give him in the twenty years which followed. He had to mature. He heeded the divine word of exhortation, 'let us . . . go on to maturity'. As with the Master, so it is with the servant.

In the 'Letter about Maturity', to the Hebrews, it is this experience of Jesus himself which is the basis for our going on to maturity. In a sense Christ's maturity is the central theme of Hebrews. But he also presented a sacrifice which was mature, or perfect — once again the same family of words is employed. He, being made mature, became the source of eternal salvation for all who obey him (Heb. 5:9), because he offered a sacrifice which was 'complete' in the sense that it was able to accomplish what the sacrifices of the Old Testament era could only symbolise, namely the forgiveness of sins and the real cleansing of the hearts and consciences of those who believe (Heb. 10:1-25). The remarkable teaching of Hebrews is that Christ has done something which is able to produce a maturity in Christians similar to the maturity of his own life and character; by his work he is able to enable us to grow in grace and favour with God.

We therefore have a two-fold motivation in Christ to press on to maturity. This is *the example he has set before us*; this is also *one of the reasons why he died for us*. We dare not therefore regard the issue as one of secondary importance. So the writer emphasises: 'We have come to share in Christ if we hold firmly till the end [literally, *to maturity*] the confidence we had at first' (Heb. 3:14).

(b) The Teaching of Paul
In the light of this, it is hardly surprising to find frequent

reference in Paul's letters to the importance of spiritual maturity.

The Corinthians

A glance at Paul's first letter to the church at Corinth indicates the extent of the anxiety they caused him. Towards the end of the letter there is a moving appeal which takes us to the heart of their problem: 'Brothers,' he says, 'stop thinking like children. In regard to evil be infants, but in your thinking be adults [literally, *mature*]' (1 Cor. 14:20). The significance of these words can easily be by-passed, set as they are in the midst of some of the most controversial passages in the entire correspondence. But they expose what had gone wrong in the lives of the Corinthian Christians.

God had given marvellous gifts to this fellowship. They lacked no spiritual gift (*charismata*) (1 Cor. 1:7). Christ their Lord had provided men to minister to them: Paul himself, the eloquent Apollos, the powerful Simon Peter (1 Cor. 1:12). But what had they done? They had divided into factions, each favouring the preaching of one rather than another (1 Cor. 1:11, 12). They did not seem to realise that these men were only servants *through whom*, and *not in whom*, they had come to believe (1 Cor. 3:5). It was not Paul, or Apollos, or Peter who was crucified for them, but Christ of whom they heard from these men's lips (1 Cor. 1:13).

God had also furnished them with gifts as well as men: prophecy, tongues, miracles, the word of faith and the word of knowledge and every other spiritual gift (1 Cor. 14:26). These had been distributed to them for the good of them all (1 Cor. 12:7). In fact these gifts were vehicles by which they could transport the love of God in their hearts in practical ways to one another. They were the hands by which believers could communicate with and minister to one another, and serve one another's best interests. They provided opportunity for practical self-denial and for esteeming others as more important than themselves (1 Cor. 12:25, 26).

But what in fact had happened? The Corinthians were boasting about these grace-gifts, and using them to further their own self-interests. 'Your boasting is not good,' says Paul (1 Cor. 5:6). In the meantime, they left unattended the pressing moral and spiritual needs of their fellowship. Despite all their gifts, there was strife, lovelessness, pride and immorality. 'You are behaving like children' was Paul's conclusion.

What had gone wrong? They did not see that both men and gifts are but the wrappings in which the parcels of God's grace are sent to us. What is of primary importance is recognising the hand that gives the gifts, and employing the gifts received for the benefit of others. To receive such gifts is to be given a special responsibility to pass on their benefits to others, but in this the Corinthians had signally and miserably failed. Like very young children when they receive a gift, the truly valuable had been abandoned to a corner and the Corinthians were taken up with the brightly-coloured wrapping paper in which it had arrived. They had lost all sense of value and proportion. It is in this context that Paul speaks of showing them 'the most excellent way' of *love* (1 Cor. 12:31ff.) — the love which gifts are given to convey, and without which the highest gifts are but a deceptive vanity. Love is Christian maturity in action:

Love is patient,
Love is kind.
It does not envy, it does not boast, it is not proud.
It is not rude, it is not self-seeking, it is not easily-angered, it keeps no record of wrongs. (1 Cor. 13:4, 5)
Love is self-denying, while the Corinthians were self-asserting.
Love does not delight in evil but rejoices with the truth.
It always protects,
always trusts,
always hopes,
always perseveres.
Love never fails. (1 Cor. 13: 6-8)
Love is reliable, while the Corinthians were unreliable.

It was because the love Paul described was a transcription of the life and character of the mature manhood of Jesus that he was so passionately concerned to see it exhibited in Corinth. The childishness of the Corinthians, coupled with their self-

satisfaction, was tantamount to denying Christ the fruit in
their lives for which he had died. The way they lived indicated
that they had not yet begun to think properly about what it
means to 'go on to maturity'.

The Philippians

How very different was the little church at Philippi! It alone
had shared in a practical way the burden of supporting the
apostle's ministry (Phil. 4:15). He longed for them with
unparalleled affection. He was sure of them in a way that he
could not be sure of others (Phil.1:3-8). And yet even in
Philippi there were signs of immaturity. There was some
division in the fellowship (2:14; 4:2), and that striving side by
side in the gospel which had once been such a marked
characteristic of their testimony was no longer present in such
considerable force (Phil. 1:27).

What had gone wrong? It may be that part of the answer is
to be found in the way in which Paul opens his heart out to
these fellow-Christians, pointing them to the grace of God in
his and their experience and the inconsistency of their present
life-style with the manner of life which faithfulness to Christ
and the gospel produces. In chapter 3:12-16, he speaks of the
way in which he presses on to the goal of Christ. He explicitly
states that *he forgets what lies behind*, and in an illuminating
phrase, encourages 'all of us who are mature' (Phil. 3:15) to do
the same. This is the mark of maturity he looks for; this
perhaps is the solvent of their present friction — forget the
past! Press on!

There are many Christians who need to heed this word.
Some Christians never seem to have anything to thank God
for but 'the day and hour they were converted'. What a tragedy
always to return to the past because we have never grown up
in what God did for us then, and to be living on past
knowledge of the blessing of God!

It is one of the characteristics of children that they often find
the past difficult to leave behind, and they cling to it rather
than venturing out on the basis of it into the future. I remember
as a youngster secretly going to our waste disposal bin where
my mother had thrown all the soft animal toys of my childhood
and recovering them under cover of darkness. How attached

we can be to the things of our childhood, and not want to devote ourselves to the challenges of the future! In particular how unwilling we can be to forget the *successes* of the past. For others the great hindrance to going on is their inability to forget, or at least put behind them, the *failures* of the past. That is equally damaging to spiritual progress because it involves a refusal to take at his word the God who has promised to put confessed sin and failure *behind him*. To fail here, not 'forgetting what is behind and straining towards what is ahead' (Phil. 3:13), is a sign of our immaturity. To be mature in our thinking includes the ability to focus our attention on fresh goals, rather than to sink in disappointment because either blessings or failures lie behind us in the past. Inevitably the spiritual value of this becomes clearest in old age; all those involved in pastoral work are struck by the difference between visiting elderly saints who, whatever sorrows may have been the lot of their lives, look forward to seeing the goodness of the Lord in the land of the living (Ps. 27:13), both in this world, and the world to come; and, on the other hand, the old man or woman who has lived and will die without faith in God, and has nothing left but the memories of the past, and the voice of a condemning conscience against which to try to justify themselves.

For Paul, therefore, maturity and progress were almost synonymous terms. The Christian who is pressing on is the one who is maturing. It is in this light we need to enquire of ourselves: Am I *pressing on* to and for Christ?

The Ephesians
It is generally recognised now that the letter to the Ephesians was originally a circular letter and the copy which has come down to us is the one which was received by the Christians at Ephesus. It is all the more significant therefore that in a general exposition, not written to meet one localised problem, the theme of spiritual maturity should play such an important role.

In Ephesians Paul indicates that the thing which links the grace of God in the gospel (chapters 1-3) to the practical outworking of the gospel in every day life (chapter 4:17-chapter 6) is the ministry of the word, through apostles, prophets, evangelists, pastors and teachers (Eph. 4:11). But what is this ministry for? It has a two-fold end in view. It equips all members of the church of Christ for service to one another, and this in turn builds the fellowship up to maturity, 'attaining to the whole measure of the fulness of Christ' (Eph. 4:13). What Paul says here has a remarkable pattern. All gifts come from one source in Christ; they are given to different individuals in order to minister to the whole body. Each member of the body of Christ, receiving this ministry, ministers in turn to other members, and the result is that individually and corporately, maturity develops.

One of the thrilling things about this passage is that we know, almost certainly, how Paul envisaged this working out in practice. As well as being an apostle and prophet, and accompanied by Timothy the evangelist, he himself had served for almost three years as pastor and teacher in Ephesus. During that time we know that he taught daily in the lecture hall of Tyrannus, possibly for five hours each day, if one ancient manuscript embodies an accurate tradition (Acts 19:9, RSV footnote). That is the equivalent of 50 years of three forty-minute sermons a week! It is not surprising therefore that a level of maturity was expected and realised among New Testament Christians that today would be regarded as extraordinary. But this simply proves the point that bringing Christians to maturity was a task which the apostles saw as fundamental and central in the work to which God had called them, and for which Christ had so obviously gifted them. We who follow on, and profess to belong to that tradition of apostolic, biblical Christianity cannot fail to be disturbed by the weakness of our vision and concern for maturity by contrast with theirs. What was a priority for them should inevitably be a priority for us also, both for ourselves and for our fellow Christians.

The Colossians

It was the abiding anxiety of Epaphras, the pastor of the Christians at Colosse, that they should 'stand firm in all the will of God, mature and fully assured' (Col. 4:12). In this he was sharing the burden of the man whose prison cell he had gone to share, the apostle Paul (4:12, 13). In his letter to his friend's congregation, Paul gives possibly his most eloquent expression to that burden. Speaking in the first chapter of the way in which he longs to exalt Christ in his preaching, he says that he does so 'that we may present everyone perfect [literally, *mature*] in Christ' (Col. 1:28). More striking however is *how* he does this: 'To this end *I labour, struggling* with all his *energy,* which so *powerfully works* in me' (Col. 1:29). Our English is too weak to convey the full force of Paul's language. He uses in the original the Greek roots of our words *energy, agony* and *dynamite.* This is what it costs the pastor's heart to bring men and women to what Christ wants them to be.

We are faced therefore with a two-fold reason to press on to maturity.

We are bound to the example of Christ. We are under the Lordship of Christ, and he is not only the author of our faith but the one who matures and perfects it (Heb. 12:2). To bring us to maturity is the object of his dying for us; it is the reason for which he gifted the church with the ministry of his word. *Maturity was the great goal of the apostles' ministry*; it ought therefore to be the goal of ours and the deep desire of our hearts. But is it? For the first obstacle to heeding the word of exhortation, 'let us go on ... to maturity', is our own unwillingness to go with Christ, to follow his example, and to submit to his disciplines.

2

Symptoms of decay

We have seen the impressive emphasis which the New Testament places on growing into Christian maturity. A closer examination of its teaching would indicate that this emphasis has a double edge to it. There can be no doubt that maturity was the positive vision and goal which these early believers had in front of them. But its need was also underlined for them by the disarray which failure to press on in grace seemed to produce in the fellowship of the church and in individual lives. Very often in the letters of Paul, for example, it was this kind of background and its accompanying danger signs which caused him to re-emphasise the fundamental structures of the Christian's life.

The presence of danger signs is also the background of the Letter to the Hebrews. A variety of theories have been held about the identity of the recipients of this letter. What kind of Hebrews precisely were they and what was their situation? There are still unanswered and perhaps unanswerable mysteries connected with these pages of our Bibles. But whatever their precise circumstances, it becomes evident early in the letter that the author was conscious of a variety of symptoms in their Christian experience and testimony which did not augur well and led him to believe that they were in considerable spiritual danger. They had not yet heeded his central exhortation to 'go on to maturity'. It is not surprising therefore that this letter is sometimes referred to as 'The Epistle of Warning'.

The exhortations to which this concern gave birth are spread throughout the chapters (2:1-4; 3:12-4:3; 4:14-16; 5:11-6:8; 10:32-39; 12:3-13; 12:14-17; 12:25-29). They repay careful study.

Four of these warning signs have an almost uncanny relevance to Christian life today and therefore, before proceeding to study maturity more positively, it will be wise for us to pause to examine ourselves in the light of them, in order to assess with the help of God where we are spiritually.

A LACK OF CONCENTRATION

'We must pay more careful attention, therefore, to what we have heard, so that we do not drift away' (Heb. 2:1). In different words this same exhortation appears again later in the letter: 'fix your thoughts on Jesus' (3:1); we are to 'fix our eyes on Jesus' (12:2); we are to 'consider him who endured such opposition from sinful men' (12:3). In fact what is being exposed is an inability to fix the heart and mind upon Christ and make him the chief object of devotion and attention. In 2:1, the writer uses a nautical expression to describe the consequences — without this concentration we simply 'flow by' or 'slip away from' Christ. No effort is required on our part, for the strength of the currents of the world around us will guarantee our departure from the moorings of the gospel.

It is worth noticing the variety of expressions the writer employs: we must *pay the closest attention* to Christ; we must *fix our gaze upon him*; we must, literally, *make our calculation about him*. One of the old writers of the seventeenth century, William Gouge, put it like this:

> The duty here intended is a serious, firm, and fixed
> settling of the *mind* upon that which we hear; a
> bowing and bending of the *will* to yield unto it; an
> applying of the *heart* to it, a placing of the
> *affections* upon it, and bringing the *whole man*
> into conformity thereunto.

That is an admirable summary and application of the
concentration which the Christian life demands. Ability to
willingly focus our gaze, fill our minds and devote our hearts
to Jesus Christ is a sign of real Christian growth. Its opposite is
a sign of immaturity.

The same is true of course in the natural realm. It is one of
the marks of children that however engrossed they may be at
times by some activity, they seem to be unable to deliberately
focus attention, control their concentration, and devote
themselves at will to a new activity.

I well remember the first time we took our children to the
cinema. We had planned a holiday treat, and part of it was a
trip to see the Walt Disney film *The Jungle Book*. We made the
mistake of going at the beginning of the supporting film. Our
then five-year old son looked at the folding seat — and
complained that it would snap him in two if he sat on it! When
we had persuaded him that it was safe and he had settled
down he whispered, 'When is *Jungle Book* coming on?' The
reply 'soon' did not satisfy him. 'I wanted to see *Jungle Book*...'
Soon the ice-cream lady appeared. 'Can I have an ice-cream?'
An ice-cream was dutifully fetched, only to be greeted with, 'I
think I'd rather have crisps.' 'When is *Jungle Book* coming on?'
'I don't like the dark;' 'when can we go home?' Every parent has
these or similar memories and knows well the inner cry of
frustration: 'Can you not settle down and concentrate?' But, of
course, it is beyond the powers of children to do so. They have
not grown sufficiently, or developed to that completeness of
personality which enables them to focus attention deliberately
on a given object or occupation. They are ruled by inner desires
rather than by external situations and duties. That is part of
their life as children.

It is here that so many Christians never seem to make much
progress. They allow themselves to be motivated and
dominated by the current temperature of their feelings, rather
than by the great realities of the gospel which will lead them
out to freer and fuller Christian living. Inevitably they lose the
power of concentration just as the Hebrews had done. They
cannot devote their attention to Christ in private or in public,
in singing God's praise or in reading his word, and a vicious
circle is set up in which they are denied and deny themselves

the nourishment which alone will bring them to adult Christian experience.

It is tempting to respond that this is to place a premium on intellectual abilities. It is often said that the mind of most of us ordinary mortals can concentrate on one object for only brief periods of time. And so we believe, until we find ourselves occasionally so engrossed in some object of interest that time appears to be the relative thing it really is. Hebrews makes it abundantly clear that concentration on Christ is not primarily a matter of the capacity of the intellect, but rather a matter of the condition of the heart. It is not because of the low level of their I.Q. that the writer warns the Hebrews of immaturity, but because they have become *dull of hearing* (5:11). It is less a matter of intellectual ability, and more a question of spiritual sensitivity.

What is the level of your spiritual powers of concentration on Christ? That is one of the acid tests of maturity.

A LACK OF APPETITE

'You need milk, not solid food ... solid food is for the mature' (Heb. 5:12-14). Once again the writer is employing a picture from the world of nature to illuminate the world of the Spirit. When we are infants we lack the capacity to digest solid foods and so we live on milk and fluids. Our systems could not receive, digest and employ meat, and the nutritious T-bone steak which would satisfy the adult would be unsuited to the child. So it is in the realm of the Spirit. It is worth noting that there are two other periods in life when we return to a milk diet — when we are ill and unable to cope with solids because of some poison in our digestive system, and when we are frail, perhaps at the very end of life, when the system no longer has the strength or energy to turn solids into nourishment, and the one thing needful for survival is the one thing we cannot perform — taking solid food.

This was the diagnosis of the Hebrews' condition. There are occasional indications that their spiritual digestive system had been polluted and that they showed indications of early senility through under-nourishment. Their condition was extremely dangerous. They had lost their appetite for Christ!

There were two apparent causes of this condition in which their appetite had been spoiled.

First, they seem to have indulged in pleasures and activities which were not illegitimate (in the sense of being explicitly forbidden by God's word), but which did not edify them and indeed tended to detract from the benefit of God's word and spoil their taste for Christ and the gospel. There is nothing morally wrong with sweets before meals, but every adult (although not every child) recognises that they do spoil the appetite and distort the sense of taste. This was the Hebrews' position. Later on in the letter the writer refers to these activities as 'weights' which held them back in the Christian race (12:1).

This is an extremely sensitive area of Christian living, and it would be inappropriate to divert our attention from the central issue of maturity with which we are concerned here. But the issue can be put in these terms: frequently a Christian who is under pressure because of some activity in his life will defend his action by saying: 'There's nothing wrong with it.' It is precisely this kind of activity and more significantly this kind of *attitude* which is exposed here as harmful to the spiritual appetite. In many areas the question 'What is wrong with it?' is muddle-headed, as Paul pointed out to the Corinthians. Their proud boast was 'All things are lawful unto me' (1 Cor. 6:12; 10:23). To this Paul responded, essentially: But this is not the relevant issue; rather let me suggest the questions you should be asking: 1. Does this *help* my Christian life? (1 Cor. 6:12). 2. Does it have a tendency to enslave me, so that I begin to *need* it? (1 Cor. 6:12). 3. Does it *edify* me, and build me up into a mature Christian? (1 Cor. 10:23). 4. Does it *advantage my neighbour*? (1 Cor. 10:24). The Christian whose predominant attitude to the life he leads is 'there is nothing wrong with it' is still self-centred, 'carnal' in the biblical terminology, and still a babe in Christ dominated by inner needs and desires rather than by the life-giving word of God.

The *second* influence which spoiled their spiritual appetite was more serious yet. Reference is made later in the letter to 'the sin that so easily entangles' (12:1). The picture of course is of the athletic stadium, of the lightly-clad athletes, bodies disciplined by exercise and consistent self-denial to run the race. Disobedience to the basic principles of physical fitness shows when the race is on. There is no victor's crown unless the athlete competes according to the rules (2 Tim. 2:5). Secret failure cannot be hidden then from the eye of the Judge. If we do not deal with indwelling sin, it will eventually deal with us, and we will have no energy for the Christian race because we have had no appetite for spiritual grace.

It is as true of the Great Physician with his children as it is of the family doctor with a sick child — the question which gives almost immediate indication of sickness or health is 'What is his appetite like?'

Are we able to take solid food, which is for the mature?

A LACK OF DISCERNMENT

The same passage which speaks about the appetite speaks also about the Christian's powers of discernment: the ability to distinguish the transient from the permanent. Later on in Hebrews 13:9 there is an indication that some of the readers had been deceived precisely in this area of their lives. Plausible but unbiblical teaching about what they should eat had led them away from Christ, and rather than being strengthened by grace, these rules and regulations had proved of no value to them. Nor were they the last to discover that some disciplines are too 'spiritual' to be Christian. It is particularly young Christians, unskilled in the *word of righteousness* (Heb. 5:13), who are liable to be deceived in this way.

But the principle enunciated in these words applies to more than blatantly false teaching. Sometimes the important distinction we need to discern is not between what is evil and what is good, but between what is comparatively harmless and what is actually valuable, between what is passing and what is lasting.

When we take little children out to shops with their birthday or holiday money we are naturally reluctant to let them loose on the toy counters. We know from long and sometimes painful experience that they are likely to be attracted and taken in by the bright, attractive toys which *profess* so much ('flies up to height of 75 feet') but *perform* so little (rarely flies more than 15 feet!) But children cannot see past the external attractions, beyond the packaging to the real value. Their slender experience leads them to believe all they see and to trust all that is promised. The same inability to discern the lasting from the ephemeral persists into adolescence and can reappear in adulthood. For one generation the most important thing in life in teenage years was a pair of blue suede shoes or a crew cut; for another a mini or maxi skirt, stiletto or platform heels. Without experience we are prey to all the changing fashions of the day. The same is true in the realm of the Spirit. Immature believers are inevitably 'tossed back and forth by the waves, and blown here and there by every wind of teaching' (Eph. 4:14).

In chapter one reference was made to the unhappy impression made by someone who went to College to 'get maturity'. The same speaker, addressing this group of young people, enthusiastically informed them that if they were not absolutely certain that they were exactly where God intended them to be that was strong evidence they should leave home and go abroad to preach the gospel. When we are protected by a little knowledge and experience of the ways of God statements like that cut little ice, and only promote a sense of concern at attributing such confusion to God, and possibly creating a painful sense of guilt and uncertainty in others. But I well remember the 'mopping up' operation which was required after that meeting to heal the wounds which had thus been unnecessarily opened. Those who were, inevitably as young Christians, immature, were tossed to and fro. What was presented seemed sacrificial, appeared to be spiritual, and was certainly exciting. The only problem was that it was not biblical. But only those with faculties trained by longer use of Scripture to distinguish good from evil would be safeguarded from such powerful winds.

The importance of this is scarcely capable of over-emphasis. The destiny which a young Christian carves out for himself or herself under the hand of God is almost invariably determined by the ability they gain to tell the difference between what brings momentary excitement and stimulation and the less spectacular day-after-day exercises of the Spirit which build Christian character and form us into the men and women whose lives make lasting impressions on society and in the fellowship of the church, because we bear fruit that remains. If we would grow to mature Christian stature we must set our hearts on long-term goals and devote ourselves privately and steadfastly to their accomplishment.

The picture-language which Hebrews uses underlines the necessity of this dogged discipline. The idea of having our 'faculties trained' is an athletic metaphor. The idea of 'practice' is that habitual, consistent training builds up strength and fitness for the contest. We are equipped to cope with the critical events of life not because of the decision of a moment, but the habits of a lifetime. It is by sowing a character, according to the proverb, that we reap a destiny. Victors' crowns are for those who, whether physically or spiritually, have kept the rules.

Are our spiritual faculties well trained?

A LACK OF TRUE WORSHIP

As the Letter to the Hebrews is brought to a conclusion, this particular symptom of the immaturity among the readers is increasingly emphasised. Their arms are feeble, their knees weak (12:12), and they need to be encouraged to 'worship God acceptably with reverence and awe' (12:28), and to 'continually offer to God a sacrifice of praise — the fruit of lips that confess his name' (13:15). Some indeed have to be advised of the danger of neglecting even to come together for the encouragement which communal worship brings (10:25).

If it is true that the age of a tree can be calculated by the number of rings of bark around it, it is certainly true that the spiritual maturity of a Christian is calculable from the character of his worship. That is why there is a melancholy strain in the title of one of the late Dr A. W. Tozer's books, *Worship — the Missing Jewel of the Evangelical Church*. A sad, but accurate title. Yet worship is the apex of all spiritual experience. This is how Dr Tozer put it:

> Why did Christ come? Why was he conceived? Why was he born? Why was he crucified? Why did he rise again? Why is he now at the right hand of the Father?
>
> The answer to all these questions is, 'In order that he might make worshippers out of rebels; in order than he might restore us again to the place of worship we knew when we were first created . . .'
>
> Now, worship is the missing jewel in modern evangelicalism. We're organised; we work; we have our agendas. We have almost everything, but there's one thing that the churches, even the gospel churches, do not have: that is the ability to worship. We are not cultivating the art of worship. It's the one shining gem that is lost to the modern church, and I believe we ought to search for this until we find it.
>
> *The Best of A. W. Tozer* p.217

It is surely not insignificant that Paul put his finger on exactly this symptom in the church at Corinth. Their maturity, he contended, was not to be judged by the number of their gifts but by their desire for the presence and power of God among them as they waited on him in worship and praise. That was the ultimate reason why the word of prophecy should have precedence over their concentration on uninterpreted tongues. Hearing tongues a stranger would think they were all mad! But if he comes in, and under the powerful prophetic ministry of God's truth the secrets of his heart are exposed, he will fall down on his face and confess that God is present among his people (1 Cor. 14:23-25). What an indictment that is of the contemporary church and some of its fascinations! Paul's whole argument proceeds on the presupposition that the first, and best, and most important concern of the church is the worshipping of God, and the sense of his presence. He is the God who was enthroned on the praises of his people (Ps. 22:3).

Is God still enthroned in our worship?

THE DANGER

Why is this matter so very urgent? We need look no further than the context of the exhortation which is the focus of our attention. One of the curious things about Hebrews 6, notoriously one of the most difficult parts of the New Testament to understand with any degree of certainty, is that in the context of speaking about *spiritual immaturity* the writer's attention seems suddenly to switch to *the possibility of apostasy*. Hebrews 6:4-6 is often discussed with this question in view: Is it possible for a true Christian to commit apostasy? But what the writer himself had in view was that there comes a time, if we persist in our immaturity, when that immaturity becomes practically indistinguishable, to ourselves and others, from actual apostasy.

Part of the background in Hebrews is the Exodus and the wilderness wanderings, the rebellion of the children of Israel and their subsequent failure to enter the land promised to them by God. Who is to say whether many of that redeemed multitude were simply showing signs of immaturity, or had gone to the extent of committing apostasy? What happened nationally and corporately can so easily happen individually!

There is a very significant example of this in the Gospels. There we are given pen-portraits of two close friends of Christ: Simon Peter who denied him and Judas Iscariot who betrayed him. But who would have said on the night of their sin, watching the remorse-filled face of Judas (Matt. 27:3) and seeing the tear-filled eyes of Peter (Matt. 26:75), that the latter had only evidenced spiritual immaturity while the former had actually committed apostasy? Both of them had failed to pay close attention to what they had heard (Heb. 2:1ff.), both had drifted out into the ocean of their own strength. Neither demonstrated visibly that he was still anchored to Christ. It apparently happened without their knowledge. It happens always like that.

Is there any difference then between immaturity and apostasy? The Gospel story hints that there is as do these powerful verses in Hebrews 6. They list what is possible to experience, and yet commit apostasy: to be enlightened, to taste the heavenly gift, share in the Holy Spirit, taste the goodness of the word of God, and the powers of the age to come. But there is no mention of what is characteristic of genuine Christian experience — fellowship with a crucified Saviour. It was this that marked the difference between Judas the apostate and Peter the immature. Judas regretted his deed, perhaps regretted that everything had fallen apart in his hands; Peter on the other hand went out and wept bitterly, and of all men that night he shared fellowship with a crucified Saviour. He wept his way from the darkness of his failure to the foot of the Cross, to his Lord, 'looking to Jesus, the author and maturer of our faith, who for the joy that was set before him, endured the cross, despising the shame, and is now set down at the right hand of the throne of God on high' (Heb. 12:2).

It may be that we also need to reflect on our spiritual condition as we are conscious that these marks of spiritual immaturity are present in our own life, that this danger is our danger. Perhaps we need to weep our way from where we are today to where Christ is and where he summons us to be.

'Brothers, I urge you to bear with my word of exhortation' (Heb. 13:22).

3

Abiding in Christ

How are we to grow to maturity? It is one thing to 'bear with this word of exhortation' (Heb. 13:22); but how are we practically to put it into effect and operation in our lives? One of the great blessings of becoming familiar with the Scriptures is that very often, indeed constantly, they provide *answers* to such questions. This should not really surprise us. After all, God himself is concerned about our progress — we are his children! And those who wrote the New Testament were not merely public persuaders but also shepherds of God's flock. Some of them were men who grew to maturity under the personal guidance of Jesus. Throughout the New Testament we would therefore expect to find echoes of his work in their hearts.

No passage deals more clearly with this theme than the words John recorded at the heart of our Lord's discourse in the Upper Room:

> I am the true vine and my Father is the gardener. He cuts off every branch in me that bears no fruit, while every branch that does bear fruit he trims clean so that it will be even more fruitful. You are already clean because of the word I have spoken to you. Remain in me, and I will remain in you. No branch can bear fruit by itself; it must remain in the vine. Neither can you bear fruit unless you remain in me.

> I am the vine; you are the branches. If a man
> remains in me and I in him, he will bear much fruit;
> apart from me you can do nothing. If anyone does
> not remain in me, he is like a branch that is thrown
> away and withers; such branches are picked up,
> thrown into the fire and burned. If you remain in
> me and my words remain in you, ask whatever
> you wish, and it will be given you. This is to my
> Father's glory, that you bear much fruit, showing
> yourselves to be my disciples.
> As the Father has loved me, so have I loved you.
> Now remain in my love. If you obey my
> commands, you will remain in my love, just as I
> have obeyed my Father's commands and remain
> in his love. I have told you this so that my joy may
> be in you and that your joy may be complete.
>
> (John 15:1-11)

It is sometimes mistakenly assumed that Jesus is urging his disciples here to *evangelistic activity*. That would be a very strange way to interpret his words in this context. Evangelism was at that period of their lives probably the last thing on their minds. Far more likely is the interpretation of these words which understands them to refer to continuing in the Christian life, and bearing the fruit of a truly spiritual character. It is this which 'proves' a person to be a disciple of Jesus Christ; not his personal gifts or influence, but his growth in grace. What did Jesus have to say about this?

SPIRITUAL GROWTH IS FOUNDED ON OUR UNION WITH CHRIST

This, of course, is the point of the illustration which Jesus uses — the allegory of the vine and the branches. The believer's life is dependent upon his relationship with Christ in a rather similar way to the way in which the branches of the vine depend upon it as the source of their life and nourishment. The picture is really a very clear one: if the branches do not remain in the vine, then instead of growth there is the beginning of a certain death. It may appear otherwise momentarily, but in time the branch fails to bear fruit, it withers and is cast aside to be burned (John 15:6).

It is quite possible for a Christian to grow in grace and in the knowledge of Christ to some extent without ever appreciating the nature of this faith-relationship. But it is a very rare thing to make real and lasting advance without grasping the wonderful truth which lies behind the picture of the vine and the branches.

There is a word used in the passage which gives us particular insight into what Jesus meant. His basic teaching is that, while he is the vine, 'you are the branches' (v.5.). 'Branches' is perhaps a misleading translation. The word used, *klēma*, really means a shoot, a young twig or in this context in all probability, a 'graft' — a shoot which has been broken of in order to be replanted or grafted into a fruitful vine. The *background* helps to explain the relevance of these words. The men who first heard them were Jews, members of Israel the Vine of God. Asaph the psalmist had sung:

> You brought a vine out of
>   Egypt;
>   you drove out the nations
>   and planted it.
> You cleared the ground for it,
>   and it took root and filled
>   the land.
> The mountains were covered
>   with its shade,
>   the mighty cedars with its
>   branches.
> It sent out its boughs to the
>   Sea,
>   its shoots as far as the
>   River.

But even Asaph has to reckon with the tragedy which had befallen this faithless vine:

> Why have you broken down
>   its walls
>   so that all who pass by pick
>   its grapes?
> Boars from the forest ravage it
>   and the creatures of the field
>   feed on it.

> Return to us, O God
>   Almighty!
> Look down from heaven
>   and see!
> Watch over this vine,
>   the root your right hand has
>   planted,
>   the son you have raised up
>   for yourself.
>
> Your vine is cut down, it is
>   burned with fire;
> at your rebuke your people
>   perish.
>   (Ps. 80:8-16)

The Prophet Ezekiel had spoken in similar terms of the vine which God planted but which proved unfaithful (Ezek. 19:10-14). Isaiah before him had sung his 'Song of the Vineyard' about the Lord of the vineyard who had 'looked for a crop of good grapes, but it yielded only bad fruit' (Is. 5:2). But now Jesus claimed to be the true vine of which the vine of the Old Testament had been the illustration. To belong to God and his people now meant being united to Christ by faith and through grace — just as the gardener might cut off a branch from an old rejected vine and graft it into the strength and nourishment of a living vine.

This picture solves one of the difficulties many Christians have felt about what Jesus says. Is it possible, it is often asked, to be in the vine and then as verse 6 suggests, to be cast off? To be a Christian one day and no longer a Christian the next? But to ask this question is to fail to grasp the picture, which is that of the Vinedresser or Gardener going round his vine to see whether his grafts have 'taken'. If they have not taken, how does he know? Jesus answers: it is the graft which does not bear fruit and therefore shows no evidence of being genuinely united to the vine which he takes away and burns.

The Christian, then, bears fruit by maintaining his relationship to Christ, so that Christ's life may be in him and may release through him God's grace and love. It is interesting to compare this, in Jesus' teaching, with a similar horticultural metaphor in Paul's teaching on the Christian's union with Christ.

In Romans 6:1-14, Paul speaks about the implications of this union with Christ. His thinking is this: If we are really united to Christ, we must be united to him in his death and resurrection, united to him as one who died and was raised. But if that is the case (which it is) we must also share in the influence this may have on our own lives — if he died to sin, and was raised to new life for God (Rom. 6:2-4), then we too must have died to sin with him, and come through to a new life of consecration to our Lord. That is a tremendously powerful truth to grasp. But the really startling thing about Paul's expression of it is that he says: 'If we have been united with him in his death, we will certainly also be united with him in his resurrection' (Rom. 6:5). The word translated 'united' in our modern versions was once thought to be derived from the verb 'to plant together', hence the AV translation 'planted together'. But in fact it is derived from a verb which means 'to grow together', and so 'to be bound up with', 'to be closely related to'. The basic meaning is 'native'. It is the verb which would be used of a characteristic with which a person had 'grown up' — a father's eyes, a mother's face and so on. Paul is therefore saying that the Christian is someone who 'grows up with' Christ's death to sin and resurrection to live for God as fundamental parts of his life — he is 'born again' with them. He does not progress to the position where sin no longer has dominion over him (Rom. 6:14). That is where he begins. He is under grace which reigns through righteousness to eternal life in Christ (Rom. 5:21). And from that position, from this new identity, he must grow and go on growing.

These twin truths, that we have been grafted by the grace of God into Christ, and that our union with Christ gives us a new relationship both to sin and to God, form a fundamental growth point in Christian understanding and living. But it is not a point on which we can linger here, except to underline the importance of grasping the truth which passages such as Romans 6:1-14; John 15:1-11; Colossians 3:1-4, and Galatians 2:20 expound. Here the Christian must also become the gardener of his own soul, and lovingly devote time to the increasing of his understanding of his fellowship with Christ. We are all tempted to quick routes and short-cuts to the truth of these passages making lasting impressions upon us, and transforming our lives. But the great lessons, like the best fruit, take time, care, thought and patience to really learn. It is a common experience for young Christians to read a book or booklet dealing with union to Christ and all the blessings which it brings and like Archimedes to rush out shouting, 'Eureka! I have found it!' But all too frequently that kind of discovery has only a passing influence. Lasting influences develop by *understanding* rather than by *feeling*.

SPIRITUAL GROWTH IS MAINTAINED BY THE FATHER'S CULTIVATION

There is something quite exquisite about our Lord's words: 'my Father is the gardener'. It is an analogy which bears almost endless practical application, reflecting as it does the constancy, patience, interest and labour which the Father bestows simultaneously on his Son and his people. We have seen the Old Testament's insight into the lavishness of God's care on the faithless Vine of Israel; how much more care does he display on the new, true vine he has planted in Christ!

In his use of the picture, however, Jesus concentrates attention on one aspect of the gardener's labours — 'every branch that does bear fruit he trims clean' (v.2). The Father *prunes* the vine. The verb means 'to clean', and clearly in this context refers to the action of 'cleansing' not by washing (as in John 13:8-11) but by cutting down and cutting back, although there seems to be no other use of the word in this sense in Greek literature. It is, therefore, a most interesting example of John saying a good deal by the use of one simple word — pruning for the Christian is a work by which an inner cleansing takes place. Leon Morris in his commentary on John's Gospel well assesses the situation: 'Left to itself a vine will produce a good deal of unproductive growth. For maximum fruitfulness extensive pruning is essential. This is a suggestive figure for the Christian life. The fruit of Christian service is never the result of allowing the natural energies and inclinations to run riot' (p.669). In the words which follow, Jesus assures the disciples that they are already clean through his word (the same words as appear in John 13:10). They have

received the washing of forgiveness; now they must receive
the cleansing of pruning.

Pruning

It is always one of the dangers of biblical exposition that in our
study of passages like this we learn more about the natural
basis of the illustration than about its spiritual significance.
How easily an exposition of Psalm 23 slips into a discourse on
the habits of near-eastern sheep and their shepherds! But the
idea of pruning lends itself to a number of valuable lessons.
The spiritual lessons we learn all fall under this general
heading: *The Father's pruning involves his providences and
interventions in our lives which make for the production of
truly Christian character.*

What lessons can we learn from this horticultural
illustration? Several basic principles of pruning give us some
guidance:

(a) The aims of pruning differ according to the stage of
development of the plant. In the early years of its life, the basic
function is not directly to produce fruit, but patiently to
prepare it for future fruit. So pruning is undertaken to create
the proper form and shape in the plant, which will fit it for its
future service. In the most general terms the same may be said
of the work of God's grace in our earliest period of Christian
living. God's purpose is to lay the foundations in our lives on
which he may build for the future. In contrast to our heavenly
Father's patience here, we tend to look impatiently for
immediate fruit, and press young Christians into a mould so
early on in their lives that their Christian growth becomes
distorted and lasting fruit is incapable of production. Perhaps
the most frightening illustration of this is the press-ganging of
fresh converts into the most public forms of Christian service
— testifying, singing, preaching the gospel and so on — when
their greatest need is to be taken and patiently shaped by the
influences of God's word and Christian fellowship. If that does
not happen, then some of the basic healing processes, the
establishing of new principles of living, the understanding of
the whole of God's word, may never emerge in the believer's
life. He will become a seven-day wonder!

Impetuous Simon Peter discovered this in his own
nurturing under the care of Christ, and gives a very basic
illustration of it in his first letter. The problem he is tackling is
this: How are young Christians, married to non-Christian
husbands, to win their husbands to Christ? It may be helpful
to pause and think about that in the form of a multiple choice
question:

> Tick the answer you would give to the following
> question put to you by a young Christian woman
> converted within the last five years:

Question: I have been a Christian for a few years. My husband
is not a Christian, and as yet shows very little interest. What do
you advise me to do?

Answer: (i) Tell him if he isn't converted by the end of the
             year, you will return to your mother.
             (ii) Send him Christian literature through the post
             in an unmarked brown envelope.
             (iii) Bear your witness to him by doing your daily
             Bible study when he can see what you are doing.
             (iv) Regularly provide him with evangelistic
             literature.
             (v) Tell him as often as you can about the
             difference Christ has made to you.

None of these answers is the one Peter gives. He sets before us
another alternative:

> (vi) 'Wives, in the same way be submissive to your
> husbands so that, if any of them do not believe the
> word, they may be won over *without talk* by the
> behaviour of their wives, when they see the purity
> and reverence of your lives' (1 Pet. 3:1, 2).

What is the principle behind these words? It is this: God
provides opportunities for preaching — and he gives men gifts
to take the opportunity; God provides opportunities for us to
speak with others about Christ — and he makes that our
responsibility and privilege. But our primary task in the
fundamental relationships of life is this: to be shaped and
fashioned in character in obedience to God's clearly revealed
will, so that his presence will shine through our transformed
lives. In other words, as husbands, wives, parents, children,
bosses, workers, our primary witness is formed by living out
in daily practice the will of God given to us in such passages as

Ephesians 5:22-6:9, and Colossians 3:18-25. How dull and unspectacular! How dreary! How painful to the flesh which has conjured up a hundred-and-one ploys to produce abundant fruit in the Christian life. Yes — says our Lord . . . My Father *prunes clean*. Our 'epistle of maturity' agrees: 'No discipline seems pleasant at the time, but painful. Later on, however, it produces a harvest of righteousness and peace for those who have been trained by it' (Heb. 12:11).

When a Christian sets his mind on these *long term goals* which God has in view, the Father comes to him, pruning knife in hand, and smilingly muses . . . 'Later on . . . a harvest; later on . . . a harvest'.

(b) The further pruning of a plant has a two-sided function. It aims to prune back the growth in order to produce a balance between *new growth* and *the production of fruit*. The husbandman is concerned for *present production*, but he is also concerned to *husband the resources* of the vine for future more mature and richer bearing of fruit. And so with great skill — though at times apparent carelessness — the strokes of his pruning knife cut down twigs, so that they lie apparently wasted around the vine. One of the skills of the gardener at such a time is his ability to distinguish between adequate pruning and over-severity. Of course a vine severely pruned will produce leaf-bearing shoots, but these invariably become fruitless stems. What may seem to be successful turns out to be counter-productive. If he cuts too far from the bud, the stub will die and harbour disease. If he cuts too close to it, the bud may be damaged. With trained eye and steady hand the good husbandman cuts cleanly, correctly — close but not too close to the bud — and produces strong, fruitful growth. And as he prunes he takes away diseased wood fit to be burned (John 15:2, 6) and cuts back branches which cross over or rub against each other.

What is the application of these principles? It is that God intervenes in our lives, bringing painful experiences, allowing us times of disappointment and sorrow, in order that there may be room for us to grow. And he does this with matchless skill. We are tested, but not beyond what we can bear (1 Cor. 10:13). We experience sorrow, but it is in order that we may be comforted (2 Cor. 1:3-11). Paul's testimony was this:

> But we have this treasure in jars of clay to show
> that this all-surpassing power is from God and not
> from us. We are hard pressed on every side, but not
> crushed; perplexed, but not in despair; persecuted,
> but not abandoned; struck down, but not
> destroyed. We always carry around in our body
> the death of Jesus, so that the life of Jesus may also
> be revealed in our body. For we who are alive are
> always being given over to death for Jesus' sake, so
> that his life may be revealed in our mortal body. So
> then, death is at work in us, but life is at work in
> you.
>
> (2 Cor. 4:7-12)

No words could more perfectly describe the work of the
divine pruning knife: 'death is at work in us' — producing 'life',
or fruit through our lives.

But if the Christian is to benefit from his experiences; if as
older Christians used to say, God is to 'sanctify to us our
sufferings' we must have two principles crystal clear in our
minds, and be persuaded of them through God's word.

(a) **There are no accidents**. Our Lord spoke these words out of
the context of his own personal experience. He was the vine,
his Father the gardener. Had he not been pruned during his life
and 'learned obedience from what he suffered'? (Heb. 5:8). Was
he not on the verge of such severe pruning that he would cry
out under its sharpness, first that he might be spared it and
then in the dreadful sense that he was God-forsaken? But he
bore more fruit through his *going* than through his *coming*. His
death was no accidental slip of the gardener's knife. Indeed it
was written in the gardener's manual of old: 'strike the
shepherd, and the sheep will be scattered' (Zech. 13:7). As it
was with the vine, so it is with the branches. One of the old
writers has a fine biblical illustration of this. Using the words
of the Song of Solomon, 'He has taken me to the banquet hall,
and his banner over me is love' (Song of Sol. 2:4): he suggests
that this is a picture of the Christian's experience, nothing may
come his way without first pressing through the banner of
Christ's love. If we are his disciples, Christ says in his teaching
in the Upper Room, we will know persecution (John 15:18-21),
and we will know sorrow (John 16:20-22). But neither of these

can cut into us, like the sharp edges of secateurs, without
God's hand steadily gripping the ends. Of this we can never
afford to lose sight.

(b) **There is no waste**. Nothing which we yield to Christ, or
which Christ takes from us is ever wasted. Rather the reverse.
To possess what Christ would not have us possess is waste, to
possess anything instead of Christ and his will is waste
(cf.Phil. 3:7-11). That is not readily visible to the eye of the
flesh. To the flesh Christ is loss and the world is gain. But the
man of faith has learned a different rate of exchange. When his
ambitions are thwarted, his own plans come to nothing, and
he feels the keen knife of God on his life, this is his security:
God does not waste, I shall not want. This is true of the church
at large. From time to time we stand silenced and stunned by
some heart-breaking event by which God's people suffer loss.
What a waste! But there is no waste in what theologians have
so wisely described as the *economy* of God. Or, at a more
personal level, something is taken from us — what a waste! —
of time, energy, finance, love or care. But *nothing* is wasted by
God. It was to this that Amy Carmichael bore witness when
she prayed:

> 'Rid me, good Lord, of every diverting thing'
> What prodigal waste it appears to be, to see
> scattered on the floor the bright green leaves, and
> the bare stem, bleeding in a hundred places from
> the sharp steel.
> But with a tried and trusted husbandman, there is
> not a random stroke in it all; nothing cut away
> which it would not have been loss to keep, and
> gain to lose.

God's pruning is purposeful. 'Every branch that does bear fruit
he trims clean *so that* it will be even more fruitful' (John 15:2).

SPIRITUAL GROWTH DEPENDS ON ABIDING IN CHRIST

To emphasise the two points we have already examined does
not yet give the full balance of Jesus' teaching. In passing we
may have noticed some emphasis on the believer's *response* to

what God does; but Jesus also emphasises our *responsibility* to grow in grace. This is achieved, he says, by 'abiding' or 'remaining' in Christ. This is a very characteristic verb in John's writings. He uses it as often as the rest of the New Testament writers put together. It is variously translated by *abide, dwell, remain,* and *continue.* Jesus' command expressed in these terms is: 'Remain in me, and I will remain in you' (John 15:4). Later on, he clarifies the meaning of this mutual indwelling:

Remain in me (v.4) = If you obey my commands, you will remain in my love (v.10)

I will remain in you (v.4) = If . . . my words remain in you (v.7).

The focus of attention, therefore, is on the words of Christ, his commands, and obedience to them. When we see this, we are almost immediately delivered from the confusion which surrounds the whole idea of abiding in Christ. It is not by a special experience that it takes place, but by a determined obedience to God's word and an opening of our hearts to Christ's commandments.

There is a parallel to this in Paul's teaching about being filled with the Spirit. Writing to the Ephesians he urges them to 'be filled with the Spirit' (Eph. 5:18). He gives no explanation of *how* this is to be achieved, and only indicates that its fruit will be found in the praises and exhortations of God's people. In the twin letter to the Colossians, in the same context (he goes on in both letters to exhort Christians to their various duties in the family and in pursuit of their vocations), Paul uses another command as the basis for the praises and exhortations of the Lord's people. 'Let the word of Christ dwell in you richly' (Col. 3:16). The equation is unavoidable: we will be filled with the Spirit insofar as we allow the word of Christ to dwell richly in us. Similarly, being filled with the Spirit *means* abiding in Christ — for it is his ministry to glorify Jesus (John 16:14). And abiding in Christ *means* allowing his word to abide in us by obedience to it. On this hangs all our spiritual responsibility. What are its implications? These are twofold:

(a) **We must let the word into our minds.** This is another of the major growth points of the Christian life. Over and over again the grasping of it has led a Christian into a new dimension of experiencing the rich joy of living the Christian life. But too often tragic ignorance of it has led many Christians to know comparatively little of the grace of God. But, are not all Christians persuaded of the importance of God's word: of daily reading and prayer, of listening to the voice of God? Indeed. But not all Christians appear to understand *how* to read God's word and apply it to their lives, sometimes employing it as a book of white magic through which God deals with us in an almost irrational way. How important it is for us to grasp that the Bible is not essentially a book on which we feed our spiritual emotions! It is a book which we hear expounded and applied, or which we expound and apply to ourselves. In this way, by correctly handling the word of truth (2 Tim. 2:15), we may let its riches *take root in our minds, mould our thinking, and consequently shape our living.*

To this theme we will return, but in the meantime perhaps this concern that the Bible be read properly can be illustrated by the experience of two people known to the writer. Neither person's experience is being caricatured — although it may be their experiences are extreme forms of an approach to reading the Bible which fails to allow Scripture to do its perfect work in the believer's life:

A young man is contemplating the possibility of marriage. In his reading of Scripture he lights on the sixteenth chapter of Jeremiah, and discovers these words leaping out of the page: 'Then the word of the Lord came to me: "*You must not marry and have sons or daughters in this place*" ' (Jer. 16:1, 2). What is he to make of this? He has already developed a close friendship which he hopes will lead to marriage. Is God now dealing with his situation in a new and unexpected way? Fortunately, the young man thinks the matter through. On what grounds did he believe God was leading him to marry? Do these seem biblical and good? Then, they continue to stand. What then does he make of the text? He recognises that it was spoken at a *particular time* to a particular *individual*. By no stretch of the imagination can it apply to all. Conceivably circumstances could arise in which it might apply — but never simply as a sentence on its own. The young man concludes that his own subconscious has brought the anxiety to the fore

— it has not been sufficiently geared yet to Scripture. Perhaps even Satan has had a hand in the experience, seeking to destroy his confidence in the will of God for his life. He moves on, therefore, a little shaken, but wiser and stronger as a result.

A mother sits reading Isaiah 47, on which she has been asked to speak at a meeting some time in the future. There are five children in the family, but they are not all with her at the moment during school and university holidays. She is reading God's word against Babylon:

> Now then, listen, you wanton creature,
>   lounging in your security
> and saying to yourself,
>   'I am, and there is none besides me.
> I will never be a widow
>   or suffer the loss of children.'
> Both of these will overtake you
>   in a moment. On a single day:
>   loss of children and widowhood.
>   (Is. 47:8-9a)

For the next two days she finds herself in considerable distress. Is this God's word to her? She cannot escape from the pressure of such a warning. Her sense of harassment is only brought to an end when she goes back to first principles of understanding Scripture. She examines the context, she compares herself with Babylon, God's enemy. But she is God's child! She realises that understood out of context these words of Scripture have bypassed her mind and gone straight to her subconscious fears. Who knows but Satan's hand has once again been present? In the light of a proper understanding of Scripture, her mind is enlarged to think of God's care for her — and peace is restored.

This pin-points the issue. Too many Christians allow their minds to be merely empty vessels to carry God's word to the *feelings*. But if that word is to bear lasting fruit, we must engage all our powers to enable us to *understand* it.

(b) **We must let the word influence our wills.** Alongside the failure to rightly understand God's word, the chief weakness of many Christian lives is the failure to bend the will in obedience to it. Not only is the *mind* often the slave of the *feelings*, but the *will* seems to be captured by them too, and the life of the Christian grows weak because he does not 'feel' so strongly as he once did. But *it should be the aim of every Christian to have his will directed by the will of God revealed in Scripture*. This leads to a life of *obedience* — and obedience in turn leads to a life of fruitfulness.

Growing a fruitful vine is not easy for the husbandman. It will have its arduous moments for the branches too. Too often we look for a kind of abiding in Christ which is at best a form of psychological relaxation, and the experience of it more akin to the effects of transcendental meditation than biblical Christian living. It is a mindless approach to God and his word which looks more for psychological release from personal tensions rather than engaging the mind to know and do God's will.

Every true Christian will want to be familiar with God's pattern for his spiritual growth. Here, in John 15, Jesus reveals it. It is based on our union with him. It is furthered by the Father's pruning. It depends on the disciple's abiding in Christ. When this is clearly fixed in our minds and our experience we will discover the lasting enjoyment of our spiritual privileges. To some of these we will turn in the chapters which follow.

Standing firm

4
Full assurance

Two problems often recur in the experience of Christian people. One is the uncertainty which some Christians experience about the reality of their faith and the genuineness of God's love from them. That is the problem of assurance. The second is the perplexity, common to younger Christians particularly, about knowing the will of God and experiencing his guidance in life. That is the problem of guidance. It is important to realise that the Bible looks on neither of these aspects of living the Christian life as problematic. Both assurance and guidance are thought of as marvellous privileges which are the common property of all the children of God. We will consider some of the biblical teaching on these themes.

THE POSSIBILITY OF ASSURANCE

The very first thing every Christian needs to grasp is that God has made it possible for his children to enjoy assurance. That is particularly important in this matter of maturity, for just as in ordinary life mature conduct, self-possession and well-balanced personalities depend on acceptance and a knowledge that others do accept us, so in the Christian life it is very difficult to grow to any degree of maturity without a basic confidence that God cares for us and that we really do belong to him. Many of the promises of the gospel would be enervated of their power and helpfulness if we have no confidence in the God who lies behind them as our own Father in heaven. Consequently a good deal of the Bible aims to produce this confidence in God and many of the personal confessions in which the Bible abounds are in fact statements of assurance. Paul often writes about how he has been 'persuaded'; how he is 'sure'; how he abounds in hope. But one of the interesting things about him is that he does not speak about such assurance with his eyes closed to the harsh realities around him. Nobody knew the harshness of life as a Christian more intimately than he did. When he spoke of his assurance that neither death nor life, angels, principalities nor powers, height, depth, nor any other creature, could ever separate him from God's love in Christ (Rom. 8:38, 39) he was speaking out of long personal acquaintance with these very antagonists of assurance. He had been imprisoned frequently, flogged five times, beaten three times with rods, experienced shipwreck, spent a night and a day in the open sea, had been in danger from rivers, bandits, Jews, Gentiles, on land, at sea, known hunger and thirst, nakedness, peril and sword (2 Cor. 11:24-29). And although in such passages as Romans 8:31-39, he has reached a pinnacle of elation, even there he simply states what he has expressed elsewhere. He knows the love of God shed abroad in his heart by the Spirit (Rom. 5:5); he is sure that Christ will keep all that he has committed to him (2 Tim. 1:12). This is commonplace for the New Testament Christian. But it is held out to us against a dark backcloth.

There is the possiblity of a false assurance. In fact one of the concerns of the New Testament is to distinguish true from false assurance. No matter what a man *professes*, it is what he *possesses* which is the acid test of his state of grace. Does he possess the Spirit of Christ? (Rom. 8:9). If not, then he does not belong to Christ! Does he show the fruit of the Spirit, or the works of the flesh?

This is even more clearly present in the ministry of Jesus. From the commencement of his ministry we find warnings about the possibility of appearing before Christ on the last day under the false assumption that fellowship with him has been long established and that service in his name passes as the ground of assurance. But on that day he says he will say to many 'Depart from me, I never knew you' (Matt. 7:21-23). Words which evoke the response 'Lord, is it I?' from every sensitive heart, and indicate that assurance is not simply a matter of our 'knowing' Christ but rather of him knowing us and of us allowing him that personal intimate knowledge of our lives which indicates our abandoning of ourselves wholeheartedly to him.

It is, in the light of this, terribly possible for someone to have a kind of faith and assurance that is little more than self-confidence, born out of an intellectual conviction (what our fathers called 'historical faith') rather than out of a helpless casting of one's sinful self upon a willing Saviour. But so long as there is a vestige of reliance on my righteousness, my service, my gifts, my knowledge of Scripture — so long as I rely on my faith rather than on Christ's work alone — so long am I the possessor of a false and temporal assurance. The sands of time are littered with the strewn wreckage of men and women who have made shipwreck of their souls because they went forward with a false assurance, not having really laid the foundation of Jesus Christ and him crucified. That is a tremendous danger.

There is the possibility of a lack of assurance. A failure to enjoy real assurance may arise from two mistakes. On the one hand we assume that it would be presumptuous to claim to have it and so we abandon one of the most gracious gifts which God holds out to all his children; or, we assume that unless one possesses full assurance it is extremely unlikely that one possesses true salvation. It ought to be made as clear as possible that a person may be a Christian, an heir of salvation, without possessing a full persuasion that God is their Father, and that Christ is their Saviour.

The simple fact is that salvation and assurance are not the same thing. Assurance is our reaction to the gift of salvation, and our reflection on our trust in Christ. Wonderful though it is, it is not necessary for justification. Faith alone justifies, through Christ alone. Assurance is the enjoyment of that justification. The *Westminster Confession of Faith* rightly says that 'A true believer may wait long and conflict with many difficulties before he be partaker of it (assurance)'. Just as some of us take much longer to adjust to the idea that someone loves us so according to our dispositions, circumstances, personalities and the providences of God we vary in the ease and the degree with which we come to enjoy abounding confidence in the salvation of God. Not only so, but assurance is subject to different degrees of intensity in different believers, and at different times in the same believer, and it is important for our own well-being and stability to recognise this.

But it is vital to balance the possiblity of true faith carrying little assurance with the further emphasis of the same *Westminster Confession* that 'such as truly believe in the Lord Jesus ... may, in this life, be certainly assured that they are in the state of grace, and may rejoice in the hope of the glory of God'. Assurance is something we should think of as normative. It is simply not God's way under normal circumstances to keep his children waiting for the light of his countenance. He has not given us a Spirit of bondage, writes Paul, but a Spirit of adoption, bringing assurance, whereby we cry 'Abba, Father' (Rom. 8:15). The words of the servant in our Lord's parable sum up this bondage frame of spirit: 'I knew you were a *hard man*.' That bondage finds an echo in the hearts of many children of God who cannot escape the fear that God, after all, holds something against them. For many Christians that spirit — the spirit of the elder brother in the famous parable of the Prodigal Son — is the greatest enemy of their enjoyment of God and the full experience of confidence and trust in his presence.

The only way for this suspicion of God to be dispelled and for a true sense of assurance to be given, is by a proper understanding of the real basis of our assurance. Only a proper understanding of *God* will give us the assurance for which we long.

THE FOUNDATION OF ASSURANCE

We have already hinted that the key passage in the New Testament on assurance is probably Romans 8. The expression of assurance comes towards the end, and takes the form of a debate or argument with anyone who would deny the child of God his inheritance. In the course of his debate, Paul lays bare the foundation stone on which he has built his own assurance. He asks four questions, each beginning with the word *Who?* and a good case can be made out for thinking that he answers them with another series of four questions. To get to the heart of Paul's argument it helps to consider his statements in the reverse order to that in which they appear in Romans 8:31-35.

v.35: Who shall separate us from the love of Christ? Shall trouble or hardship or persecution or famine or nakedness or danger or sword?

v.34: Who is he that condemns? Christ Jesus, who died — more than that, who was raised to life — is at the right hand of God and is also interceding for us.

v.33 Who will bring any charge against those whom God has chosen? It is God who justifies.

v.32: He who did not spare his own Son, but gave him up for us all — how will he not also, along with him, graciously give us all things?

v.31: If God is for us, who can be against us?

In verse 35, Paul presents the possibility of *final separation* and lists the variety of powers and influences which, on the surface, seem capable of destroying both life and faith in Christ. He mentions the experiences which many Christians most dread, and imagine are likely to destroy their bond with Jesus. Trouble! Hardship! Persecution! Hunger! Nakedness and cold! Danger! Death! Not only are these *potential* trials but *already* they are being experienced by God's people (8:36). What is he to say in the face of all this which militates against the confidence in Christ he is professing? Precisely that *in all these things Christians are more than conquerors in Christ!*

It is one thing to say that or more probably to find yourself saying it to a beleaguered fellow Christian. But what sense does it make? Is it not really burying our heads in the sand? Of course not! What Paul means to say is that *in all these things we are not removed from Christ and his love. It would be false* logic to think so. Does a father love and care less for his child because that child is in difficulties? The idea defies family logic! But Paul says more, for in these things Christians are 'more than (= super) conquerors'. How does this come about? Because as he explains in verse 39, these powers which range themselves against us cannot separate us from God's love in Christ. They made their greatest concerted effort to do so when *he* was crucified, but they failed. Now his love for us is beyond their reach, and we are therefore not only conquerors but so certain is the victory and the conclusion foregone that we may think of ourselves as 'super-conquerors'.

In verse 34 another threat appears. Condemnation! 'Who can condemn us?' We miss the force of what is said if we assume Paul's answer is 'nobody'. That is not his position. On the contrary, there is someone who can condemn — Jesus Christ. It is he who has the power to say 'depart from me, ye cursed, into everlasting fire, prepared for the devil and his angels' (Matt. 25:41AV). He himself claimed to be the possessor of all authority in heaven and on earth (Matt. 28:18), but also the one into whose hands all judgment had been committed (John 5:22). He is surely well able to condemn, and when we stand before him in his holiness, we recognise how justly we deserve condemnation. But Paul affirms that the Christ who might condemn died for us and rose again that he might not condemn us. He does not condemn at God's right hand, but serves as our heavenly advocate and intercedes for us. Nothing could be further removed from his purpose than to *condemn* those for whom he died.

Verse 33 refers to the fear of accusation. 'Who will bring any charge against those whom God has chosen?' The same verb is translated elsewhere in the AV as 'call in question' (Acts 19:40) and that well expresses the idea. Is it not possible that, for all the favour and blessing of God the Christian may have experienced, he will yet be 'called in question'? Anyone who has known what it is to be doubted by friends, to have a question mark hanging over their trustworthiness, knows what an all-pervasive sense of disquiet and uncertainty that brings. Those who have experienced any degree of what the New Testament calls the conviction of sin are able to recall the painful sense of uncertainty about one's whole life which arises when God *does* call our lives into question and leaves us without a leg to stand on. It is a bitter discovery to find that all our righteousness is a filthy rag in God's sight (Is. 64:6)!

But what is the answer to this fear, or more precisely, what answer is there to it which will guarantee me assurance of God's love? Paul's reply is that this God, who has the power and the right to call our lives into question, is the 'God who justifies'. This, in fact, is the picture of God he has been presenting throughout the letter; 'grasp the message of this letter' he is saying 'and assurance will come'. Our need then is to allow the teaching he has given to dominate our thinking about God:

> He justifies the ungodly (Rom. 4:5).
> He justifies because of Christ's righteousness and sacrifice, not because of ours (Rom. 3:21-26).
> He justifies those who have faith (Rom. 3:28).
> He justifies once, for ever, and perfectly so that we have peace with God (Rom. 5:1).

Study these chapters. There is no more common reason for lack of assurance than a wrong understanding of justification by faith. Properly understood it will be to you, as Martin Luther the great Reformer said it was for him, 'the very gate of heaven'!

Verse 31 presents a final hurdle to the enjoyment of assurance. The fear of *opposition*. 'Who can be against us?' That is not exactly how Paul puts it. He actually says: '*If God is for us*, who can be against us?' It is not in doubt that God is for us. Nor is it in doubt that we have opposition, for Paul describes it in the same breath. What Paul means is that in the light of the fact that God is for us what does the opposition we face really add up to?

If we are to be realistic we ought to recognise that in fact it adds up to a very great deal. Our Lord's parable of the sower and the soils suggests that many professing disciples have come to nothing with less opposition than that catalogued here. How can we say that such opposition is not to be feared? Paul's answer is to be found in his earlier words: 'we know that in all things God works for the good of those who love him, who have been called according to his purpose' (Rom.

8:28). God uses the very things which seem to be bent on
destroying his grace in the lives of his children — in order to
further his own purposes in them. Assurance comes, and
grows, when our hearts and minds are fixed on these truths,
until we are persuaded that this is the kind of God who in
Christ has become our Father.

Paul, however, is not content to leave things there. He finds
in the gospel that God has provided a *guarantee* of this. His
words are in the form of a logical argument — what the
logicians call an *a fortiori* argument, one in which we argue
from the stronger to the weaker. He argues thus: If God did not
spare his own Son, but delivered him up for us all, surely he
will withhold no lesser gift which is for our blessing. God has
given us his very best gift, in Christ; how uncharacteristic it
would be for him to withhold anything from us which would
help us, or to give us what, ultimately, is not calculated to
bring us nearer to him and make us more like Christ.

The Cross of Christ is God's assurance to me. It gives proof
of his grace, in that, like Abraham, *he did not spare his own
Son* (the Greek of Romans 8:32 is exactly the same as the
Greek version of Genesis 22:12) in whom alone the promises of
God were to be fulfilled. Instead, God delivered him up. While
the Gospels tell us he was delivered up by Judas, the chief
priests and rulers, and by Pontius Pilate (Matt. 26:15; 27:2;
27:26), Paul penetrates to deeper mystery yet. Christ was
delivered according to the plan of God (Acts 2:23). It pleased
the Lord to bruise him. He has put him to grief (Is. 53:10). What
further persuasion could God give you of his love?

We have not yet exhausted the importance of this teaching
for our enjoyment of the assurance of salvation. For assurance
is not merely a matter of right thinking — of theology. It is a
matter of right experience — of psychology. It is possible to
understand these truths doctrinally and yet to remain without
the enjoyment of assurance. That is why the picture Paul
presents in Roman 8 is not of Christ as Prophet, speaking
God's *word* to us, nor of Christ as King, *ruling* over us, but of
Christ as High Priest, identifying himself with us in our
weakness, need, suffering and sins, and sympathising with us.
The same picture occurs in the Letter to the Hebrews. It is
because we have a High Priest like Jesus that we can draw

near to God in 'full assurance of faith' (Heb. 10:22). He shared our frailty and our temptations (Heb. 2:10-18); he sympathises with us in our weakness, because he has shared in it (Heb. 4:14-16); he learned obedience through what he suffered (Heb. 5:7-10); and clothed in his humanity he now lives for ever to save us completely (Heb. 7:23-25). We therefore have confidence to approach God because of the flesh and blood which he shared with us and sacrificed for us (Heb. 10:19-20). It is as the *sympathetic* High Priest that Christ brings us assurance — as, in Paul's words, the one 'who loved us' (Rom. 8:37). By approaching such a Saviour, abandoning all self-assurance in coming to him as those who need him for salvation, trusting in him as the one who understands and cares, we will discover ourselves increasingly drawn near to the heart of God's love. For of him it is written:

> A bruised reed he will not break,
> And a smouldering wick he will not snuff out.
> (Is. 42:3)

OBSTACLES TO ASSURANCE

We will not travel far on the Christian pilgrimage before we discover that our experience of assurance is liable to increase and decrease from time to time, even from day to day and hour to hour. Once again those men who gathered at the Westminster Assembly wisely wrote, 'True believers may have the assurance of their salvation divers ways shaken, diminished, and intermitted.' It is important to be familiar with some of the things which can spoil our enjoyment of close communion and assurance. We should not be surprised to discover that already in Romans 8, before he breaks out into his eulogy of praise in his enjoyment of assurance, Paul had spoken of three main hindrances to it.

(a) **An inconsistent Christian life.** In the opening verses of chapter 8 Paul had described the differences between the non-Christian man and the Christian man, what he calls 'the natural man' and 'the **spiritual man**'.

The natural man:

> lives according to the flesh (v.4)
> sets his mind on the things of the flesh (v.5)
> is a debtor to the flesh (v.12)
> does not submit to God's law (v.7)

The spiritual man:

> lives according to the Spirit (v.4)
> sets his mind on the things of the Spirit (v.5)
> is a debtor to the Spirit (v.12)
> finds the law's requirements fulfilled in his life (v.4)

Paul works out this contrast in order to indicate the radical differences between the Christian and the non-Christian. But what concerns him particularly is that the Christian may take lower ground than that on which the grace of God makes him stand. He may live according to the principles which govern the life of the natural man. His true identity will then be obscured by the inconsistency of his life; first from others, but soon from himself, so that he is no longer certain whether he is a genuine Christian or not.

Later on in the Letter to the Romans Paul summons them to put on the Lord Jesus Christ, to live like him, to wear his character in life because they are united to him in spirit, and make no provision for the flesh and its passions (Rom. 13:14). Such inconsistency would be fatal to assurance. How can we be sure of a salvation which is not presently functioning in our lives?

It is axiomatic then that we cannot enjoy a high degree of assurance if we persist in living at low levels of obedience. When such inconsistency gains the ascendency there is only one possible remedy: we must mortify the deeds of the flesh. Only those who do this are assured that they are sons of God (Rom. 8:13, 14). Assurance often accompanies a single-minded resolve to deal thus with our sinful inconsistencies. By the same token the double-minded man who cannot make up his mind to devote himself wholly to following Christ is unstable and lacks assurance in all his ways (Jas. 1:8).

(b) **Failure to appreciate the indwelling of the Spirit.** What Paul describes as 'the spirit of bondage', the feeling that God is 'a hard man' is an immense hindrance to assurance. Conversely, the experience of the presence of the Spirit of adoption or sonship is a chief encouragement to confidence in God. It is important therefore when assurance is in decline not only to examine the consistency of our lives, but, in the words of Henry Francis Lyte, to:

> Think what Spirit dwells within thee
> What a Father's smile is thine.

God has not given us a spirit of slavery and bondage, but a spirit of sonship by whose presence we turn to God and call him 'Abba', Father. But how does this promote assurance? Because the Spirit *bears witness* with our spirits *that we are children of God.* What does this mean in practice? John Owen, the great Puritan preacher and writer, has a beautiful illustration in one of his books which gives us a vivid picture of this experience. The Christian, he says, is like a plaintiff in a court of law. He is trying to prove his right, perhaps to certain possessions. He puts forward his arguments as best he can, producing the evidence he has and pleading his case. But then comes the opposing counsel; arguments are brought against him, witnesses are called to oppose him; soon he doubts whether he can ever triumph in the case, and he begins to despair. But then into the court and to the witness box comes a person of undoubted integrity, who bears witness to his position, who agrees with his evidence and confirms his plea. And so the man's position is vindicated, his confidence returns, and he is once more assured of his position and his possessions.

So it is with the Christian. As he reflects on his status before God, he is able to bring forward reasons for believing he has true faith in Christ. But as he does so there are other voices raised against his in the courtroom of his heart: *Law* accuses him for his failure to keep it; *Conscience* joins the witnesses for the prosecution condemning his sinfulness; and *Satan* makes capital out of his weakness, reminding him of long-forgotten words, deeds and thoughts which seem scarcely consistent

E

with the profession he is making. Then all these voices are
silenced by the entry of the Holy Spirit. By his immediate
presence and power, by his application of Scripture to our
minds we find our case is successful. We are sure God is our
Father. And the opposition of the prosecution is dismissed.
Our integrity as true Christians is vindicated.

That this is the picture Paul employs is borne out by the
language he uses. It is sometimes suggested that the witness of
the Spirit is an experience of quiet restfulness. But that may be
to confuse the *results* of the Spirit's presence with his actual
work. For the word that Paul uses is that the believer *cries*
'Father'. The verb *krazein* is a loud, deeply emotional cry. It is
used of the squawking of a bird. It is the cry of a fallen child for
its parents. It points to the difference between the Christian
under pressure, and the non-Christian in similar
circumstances. The latter may cry 'O God, help me'; but the cry
of the believer is 'Father!' That is the supreme mark of God's
children and it shines most clearly, with the help of the Spirit,
in our darkest hours.

(c) **The Perplexity of our Afflictions.** Suffering, in whatever
form, is often thought to be one of the great objections to
believing that God is a caring Father and a hindrance to the
Christian's assurance. The Bible does not close its eyes to the
problem. The Psalms are full of heart-rending cries by men
who feel that God has deserted them and their assurance lies
in the dust around them. With great honesty the Gospel
writers record that on the Sea of Galilee, the frightened
disciples awoke Jesus in the storm, demanding '*Do you not
care if we perish?*'

Sometimes we share that questioning and complaining
spirit. 'You lifted me up', we say with one psalmist, 'but now
you have thrown me down' (Ps. 102:10). We inevitably see
affliction or trial as potentially destructive of any assurance,
because it so obviously militates against God's saving
purpose. No wonder Paul says we 'groan inwardly' (Rom.
8:23).

But in fact Paul means something quite different. He will not
endorse this view of tribulation because it is not the Biblical
perspective on it. For rather than *destroy* the purposes of God,

afflictions are part of those purposes and will therefore build rather than demolish assurance of salvation. 'For our light and momentary troubles are achieving for us an eternal glory that far outweighs them all' (2 Cor. 4:17). This is why believers 'groan' (Rom. 8:23). We catch the real sense of this experience when we notice that Paul says that the groaning of the Christian is shared by the creation (8:22) and by the Spirit (8:26). But the Spirit is groaning for answers to prayer; the creation's groans express its longing to share in the liberty of the glory of God's children. And the believer groans *as one who possesses the firstfruits of the Spirit* and longs for more of the same (8:23). Present afflictions are but the pathway to that full salvation, instruments taken up by the hands of a loving Father and employed with gracious dexterity, to fashion his children as a wood-carver's knife shapes and moulds the glory of his work of art. We can trust ourselves to Christ's knife upon us, whether as surgeon to heal us, or as craftsman to shape and mould us into his own image.

It is encouraging to notice how wonderfully Simon Peter learned this lesson. Terrified in the boat in the Galilean storm, he shared in the fear of his fellow disciples that Christ did not care. But later, endowed with the Spirit of adoption, facing a no-less severe crisis, imprisoned by Herod and awaiting probable execution, when God sent his angel to rescue him from the jaws of death how did God's servant find the apostle? In the midst of his tribulations he was enjoying his Master's assurance. He was sleeping (Acts 12:6)!

That possibility of knowing Christ's own peace in our lives is what is held out to us. But it is experienced only in a consistent Christian life, by those who are conscious of the presence of the Spirit's witness and recognise that all afflictions come to us *via* our heavenly Father.

THE MARKS OF ASSURANCE

When we enjoy assurance of salvation, what is it that captures our attention? It is the assurance that God works for our present good (Rom. 8:28); that he has a continuing purpose for the whole of our lives (v.29); that he has made complete

provision for our final salvation (v.30). Those he has
predestined he calls, justifies and glorifies. And the assurance
which these facts encapsulate is unmistakable. It may come in
different ways: as we study God's word privately; as we sit
under the ministry of the word; as we pray and worship. It
may come through obvious use of the means of grace when we
are, as it were, in its way; or it may come when we do not
expect it. Some discover assurance after long battles, others
never know what it is to be without it; for some it comes
through sorrows, for others through joys. It is as individual as
it is sovereign, and necessarily so, because it leads us to say
'The Son of God, who *loved me* and gave himself *for me*' (Gal.
2:20). But individually experienced though it is, the assurance
of salvation is always evidenced by four marks of its presence:
(i) It is accompanied by satisfaction with God's way of
salvation. The humbling of our sinful hearts before a crucified
Saviour becomes the most important thing in our experience,
whereas before it simply revealed a root of bitterness and
antagonism against the wisdom and grace of God.
(ii) It brings a new sense of security which in turn is a spur to
our duties. Paul laboured more than all — but it was not he. It
was the grace of God given to him (1 Cor. 15:10).
(iii) It fills our hearts with Christ. He is not only the foundation
of assurance, but he is himself the stream from which we daily
drink. He it is who quenches our thirst. Assurance of salvation
is assurance of Jesus.
(iv) It produces a holy boldness in our lives which is the stamp
of those who reign in life by Christ Jesus and have begun to
appreciate what it is to be more than a conqueror of sin and
Satan and all the powers of hell (Acts. 4:13, 29, 31; Phil. 1:20; 1
Tim. 3:13).

Surely this is one of our greatest needs! Let us look for it,
pray for it as a grand possibility, and enjoy it ourselves. Or
better, let us look to *him*, and pray to know more of *him*, so that
we may experience in ever more profound ways that his
banner over us is love.

5

Clear guidance

Sometimes the incidental verses of Scripture shed considerable light on the Christian life. Epaphras, for example, servant of the Colossian church prayed that his fellowship might 'stand firm in all the will of God, mature and fully assured' (Col. 4:12). These words summarise this whole section of our study of Christian maturity. It consists of two elements: *being fully assured*, and therefore encouraged to serve the Lord increasingly, and *standing firm in all the will of God*, knowing his guidance, and as a direct consequence, growing in assurance and service.

It is often suggested by commentators that Epaphras was probably a pastor of the Colossian church. The fact that he was 'always wrestling in prayer' for them certainly bears out that suggestion. The *content* of his praying emphasises this pastoral burden. For there are few more common pastoral problems, perhaps especially among young people, than 'the problem of guidance'. If we are to grow into mature Christians who are not 'infants, tossed back and forth by the waves, and blown here and there by every wind of teaching' (Eph. 4:14) it is of vital importance for us to have clear views of how God guides his people. *That* he does so is not open to dispute. It is not possible to read through the history of Israel, the personal reflections of the psalmists, the life of Jesus and the apostles, without being totally persuaded that God guides his people. At the Exodus, God 'brought his people out like a flock; he led them like sheep through the desert. He guided them safely, so they were unafraid' (Ps. 78:52, 53). The shepherding of God's people, in this sense of guidance, became a constant feature of his care for them thereafter. For this purpose he sent shepherds to teach and nourish them with guidance; he sent Christ to be the great shepherd of the sheep; he sent the Holy Spirit to guide men into all truth (John 16:13). It is clearly one of the chief benefits of the Christian life that God guides his people. But from a personal and practical point of view the real blessing of guidance is as an aid to stability, and maturity is found only when we have gained an assurance that God will guide us, and some general understanding of how he will do so.

HOW DOES GOD GUIDE?

There are two immediate problems which face us in knowing how God guides us. The first is that there is inevitably an element of mystery in God's dealings with us. His thoughts are not like our thoughts. They are higher than ours, says Isaiah, as high as heaven is above earth (Is. 55:8, 9). Of course Isaiah is thinking about salvation, for God's grace in freely pardoning us (Is. 55:7) is a reversal of all we would naturally think he would do. But he does not lose this mysterious character when he guides us. He is full of surprises. Not only so, but as God guides us, one of the things we discover is the sacred mystery of our own lives. Sometimes what God has put into us in the way of gifts or calling or destiny may take our breath away. But furthermore, to add to this there is at work what the Bible calls 'the mystery of iniquity' (2 Thess. 2:7). The book of Revelation describes the activity of a beast that has the horns of a lamb, but which speaks with the voice of a dragon (Rev. 13:11), and his presence in the lives of Christians need to be recognised, for he appears to have some of the characteristics of Christ, the true lamb of God; indeed he deliberately disguises himself in order to lead Christians astray (cf. Rev. 13:11-13 with 2 Cor. 11:14). Sometimes we are deceived by appearances, when God has commanded us to listen to voices (cf. Rev. 13:11b with John 10:3-5).

The *second* problem is this. By and large there are two quite different ideas of how God guides us, held with equal sincerity and conviction by Christian people. This is further complicated by the fact that both views can point to different parts of the Bible and claim its precedence for the position adopted. From time to time these two views clash. There is a very interesting example of this in the Diary of the famous Jonathan Edwards, the New England minister who saw several revivals take place in his congregation in the eighteenth century. During that period, George Whitefield, the great 'Methodist' evangelist, made several journeys to preach in New England, and was given overnight hospitality by the Edwards. Their impressions of this meeting were recorded by both men — and it is interesting to notice the things which Edwards mentions which Whitefield did not record. Edwards' biographer records that:

> While they were thus together, he (Edwards) took an opportunity to converse with Mr Whitefield alone, at some length, on the subject of *impulses*, and assigned the reasons which he had to think that he gave too much heed to such things.

Whitefield, in other words, was persuaded that the guidance God gave him often came suddenly and immediately into his mind. God would say to him, he believed, 'Do this' — and such a strong *impulse* in his mind and heart Whitefield felt he must obey, or he would be disobedient to his Lord.

Whitefield was not the only great Christian to hold this position. It has been common for Christians to believe that guidance from God is generally given in this way. Amy Carmichael of Dohnavur, that remarkably talented and much-used missionary servant whose life story every Christian should read seems to have held a similar view of how God guides us, and the whole story of Dohnavur would certainly seem to validate the rightness of her understanding.

On the other hand, greatly respected Christians (like Jonathan Edwards) have been uncomfortable, to say the least, with such a strong emphasis on subjective impulses and impressions. It would be possible to fill a book with stories of how easily these impressions get out of hand. What guarantee

do we have, after all, that they come from God, and are not
either irrational impulses of our own, or even of Satan? How
can we distinguish between our own personal wishes and
ideas, which often come to us suddenly and spontaneously, so
it seems, and the voice of God revealing his will? This is
possibly one of the most important of all questions in
connection with the guidance of God. We have to ask if there is
some way of understanding the teaching of the Bible which
makes sense of different Christians' genuine experience, but at
the same time is true to what we find Scripture actually
teaches.

Having begun this chapter by noticing Epaphras' prayer for
the Colossians, it may be of value to continue it by studying
Paul's prayer for them. There can be little doubt that it was
influenced by what Epaphras had told him about the basic
needs of the Colossian Christians:

> For this reason, since the day we heard about you,
> we have not stopped praying for you and asking
> God to fill you with the knowledge of his will
> through all spiritual wisdom and understanding.
> And we pray this in order that you may live a life
> worthy of the Lord and may please him in every
> way: bearing fruit in every good work, growing in
> the knowledge of God, being strengthened with all
> power according to his glorious might so that you
> may have great endurance and patience, and
> joyfully giving thanks to the Father, who has
> qualified you to share in the inheritance of the
> saints in the kingdom of light. For he has rescued
> us from the dominion of darkness and brought us
> into the kingdom of the Son he loves, in whom we
> have redemption, the forgiveness of sins.
>
> (Col. 1:9-14)

PREREQUISITES TO KNOWING GOD'S WILL

We have seen that one of the needs of the Colossians Epaphras
had shared with Paul was that of being assured of the will of
God (Col. 4:12). This is part of that maturity which Paul saw as
the temporal goal of his ministry and for which he agonised in
the energy of the Holy Spirit (Col. 1:28). But in the course of his

teaching on knowing the will of God, he emphasises two prerequisites which stand at the doorway to the revelation of that will for an individual's life.

The first is *forgiveness and redemption* (vv. 13, 14). We can be in the way of knowing the will of the Lord for our lives only when we have recognised and joyfully accepted his will *for our salvation*. It is Christ's sheep who hear his voice and recognise his accent (John 10:27). It is not at all uncommon for people to be in a tangle about the will of God for their lives, careers, families and so on for the fundamental reason that they have never come to that basic and *universal submission* to the will of God for their salvation. He wills all men *to be saved*, and it is from that entrance that the pathway of guidance leads.

Only then is a man free for God's guidance. By nature he is enslaved to the world, the flesh, and the devil (Eph. 2:1-3). It is plain in Scripture and experience how contradictory the guidance of these powers is from that of God's grace. The world offers an alternative way to the cross; the flesh lusts after wrong ways, and the devil deceives us about the true way.

Furthermore, only then is a man brought out of the darkness (Col. 1:13). One of the saddest things the Christian counsellor can hear is 'I used to think like that too, but *I don't see it* that way any longer'. That is what is so awful about the darkness out of which grace delivers us. It blinds men to the true directions of God's word. But it is tragically easy to slip back into it.

Paul also speaks in this context about being delivered out of darkness into the *kingdom* of Christ (Col. 1:12, 13). Where Christ's guidance is given, there is a kingdom, a reign, a sovereign rule. And this pin-points one of the great issues of guidance. Do I myself want guidance or advice about what I should do; or am I most deeply concerned about discerning and doing the will of God? *All too frequently all that is sought is immediate alleviation from a pressing difficulty and not a wholehearted, lasting submission to the whole will of God.* But salvation is nothing if it is not this, and that is why it is such a vital prerequisite to guidance.

But, perhaps a little curiously at first glance, the *second prerequisite* Paul mentions is *strength and might* (Col. 1:11).

This is part of his prayer for those whom he longs to bring to the knowledge of God's will.

But why strength and might? It is for what he calls 'endurance and patience'. He uses two Greek words *hupomonē*, which refers to endurance under trials, and *makrothumia*, which conveys the idea of patience under persecution by men. Paul combines these ideas on several occasions in his letters (2 Cor. 6:4, 6; 2 Tim. 3:10). It is valuable to notice that the same combination of words reappears in James 5:10, 11, where James urges both graces on his readers, following the examples of the prophets (*makrothumia*) and Job (*hupomonē*). But it is the reason and ground of this exhortation in James that is so illuminating: 'You ... have seen what the Lord finally brought about (literally, 'the end' = *telos* of the Lord]'. Here then is why the strength and might of God are so necessary in our guidance. It is because the end or purpose of the Lord in our case is sometimes no more apparent than it was to Job or the prophets. It is only visible and sometimes very dimly to the eye of faith that looks forward in the assurance that God works together all things for the good of his people. If the vision tarries there is only one proper response: we must wait for it (Heb. 2:3).

All this should help us to see that the guidance which God graciously gives is not to be separated from what we are day by day as his children. It is provided in that context; indeed it is shaped and fitted in his wisdom to our growth in grace and wisdom. It is surely a legitimate interpretation of the Fatherhood of God that his ways of guiding us may even vary according to our maturity. The fact that we are, as new born babes, ignorant of the spiritual world into which we have been born and relatively incapable of understanding fully the mystery of his ways, does not mean that he refuses to lead and guide us. Many Christians can look back with trembling wonder that when they knew so little of the will of the Lord he seemed to guide them in a sovereign way that they would not now expect him to do. So the father carries his infant on his shoulders — but not when he is a teenager!

These general considerations bring us more immediately to consider what Paul has to say about:

THE CHARACTER OF GOD'S WILL

If one danger in our thinking about guidance is to contemplate it as though it could be compartmentalised and unrelated to the rest of our Christian experience, the other is to think of guidance only in terms of our own needs and circumstances rather than from the perspective of the character of God's will. The truth of the matter is that as we learn what the will of God is in general terms so his guidance becomes clearer and more sure. *The great need we have is familiarity with how God sees things* and about this Paul has four fundamental things to say.

(a) The will of God is practical and moral

The first fruit of knowing God's will is *doing* it, 'walking worthy of the Lord' (Col. 1:10). The same emphasis appears in the twenty-third Psalm. God leads men in paths of righteousness (Ps. 23:3). It can scarcely be over-emphasised how necessary this perspective is. We can search the indices of the works of great Christian writers of previous centuries in vain for discussions on 'the problem of guidance'. They had little to say about it. Their perspective was vitally different. They asked another question: 'What can I do to please the Lord? — for *that* is my guidance.' More confusion is to be found here than almost anywhere else. But Paul states the true position with great clarity to the Romans. It is in practical yielding to God that we discover his will to be good, perfect and acceptable. It is those who deny self, giving themselves sacrificially to God, who, by the renewing of their minds, find the will of God to be good, perfect and acceptable (Rom. 12:1, 2). Guidance is not normally ecstatic or mystical. It is *always* ethical and intensely practical.

(b) The will of God is reasonable

We might almost say 'rational', for Paul speaks about the 'knowledge' of his will, and about the 'wisdom' and 'understanding' involved in it. While this does not set a premium on our intelligence, there is certainly a value placed on the use we make of our minds, and this in turn creates important implications for guidance:

(i) *We cannot be guided solely by traditions.* Guidance from tradition leads to bondage to tradition. This is not to despise tradition. Paul congratulates the Corinthians for their adherence to certain traditions (1 Cor. 11:2), but he wants them to know (see, discern, understand) the great principles which lie behind the traditions. What sad disarray our churches find themselves in because the traditions have been followed slavishly or thoughtlessly.

(ii) *We must not be guided by unthinking rejection of traditions.* We need to take note of this especially today. There is a spirit of anti-traditionalism abroad in our world, and it has had its own influence already on many Christians. When that spirit takes hold of us it is the easiest thing in the world to reject the applications of the gospel which were made by a previous generation. We can easily arrogantly assume that wisdom has begun with us and that all past tradition is empty formalism. In fact much of it has its roots in consecrated living for Christ, and it would be a disastrous principle of guidance to overthrow some of the old paths merely because they are old. In asking ourselves how contemporary Christians should respond to established traditions we need to ask only whether Christ and his cross and his word are present. If the answer is 'yes', then we must direct our lives in such a way that we earn the apostolic benediction that we 'hold to the teachings' (1 Cor. 11:2).

(iii) *We must not be guided by subjective impressions only.* Guidance does not normally by-pass the mind. Indeed it never does, strictly speaking, hence Paul's exhortation not to be 'foolish' (*aphrones* = mindless) but 'understand what the will of the Lord is' (Eph. 5:17 AV). This is an especially important word of caution to believers who are prone to 'impressions'. These are not necessarily irrational, as we will see presently, but they need to be tested, for this reason if no other that the devil is able to make 'impressions'. The great maxim then is this: 'Think it over ... and the Lord will give understanding' (2 Tim. 2:7).

(c) **The will of God is spiritually discerned**
Paul's prayer is that men may be filled with the knowledge of God's will in all wisdom and spiritual understanding. In all

probability 'spiritual' qualifies both wisdom and understanding. Along with insight (Eph. 1:18) these were the great *intellectual virtues* of Greek philosphy according to Aristotle. But for Paul they are *spiritual graces*, and consequently require the help of the Holy Spirit for their employment. This is the great balance to the emphasis on the use of the mind. It is also necessary to be sensitive to the Spirit of God. That does not mean thought is abandoned. But it does mean thought on its own is insufficient.

It is at this point that Christians who emphasise the use of Scripture and denigrate 'impressions' can go awry. There is something deeply satisfying in the knowledge that Scripture and the doctrine it teaches is sufficient for life and godliness. But here lies the danger of arid rationalism, indeed of intellectualism, since the Scripture itself teaches us never to separate the *once-for-all* given word of God from the *continuing influence* of the Holy Spirit. The application of biblical principles to daily life is therefore a matter for which we are wholly dependent upon a supernatural God, and it is in this context that every believer experiences the impressions made by God's truth on his own being, and finds it necessary to pursue them. These ought not to be discounted.

Some Christians may feel this is a betrayal of the sufficiency of Scripture. But we would be wise to notice what John Murray has to say:

> as the Holy Spirit is operative in us to the doing of God's will, we shall have feelings, impressions, convictions, urges, inhibitions, impulses, burdens, resolutions. Illumination and direction by the Spirit through the word of God will focus themselves in our consciousness in these ways ... We must not think, therefore, that a strong, or overwhelming feeling or impression or conviction, which we may not be able at a particular time to explain to ourselves or others, is necessarily irrational or fanatically mystical ... In many cases such a feeling or impression is highly rational and is the only way in which our consciousness, at a particular juncture, can take in or react to a complex manifold of thoroughly proper considerations. In certain instances it may take us a long time to understand the meaning or implications of that impression.
>
> *Collected Writings* 1:188

And if we ask how such impressions are to be progressively
understood, the fourth dimension of the will of God points us
to the answer:

(d) The will of God is biblically unfolded

Where does the wisdom and understanding of which Paul
speaks (Col. 1:9) arise? The ancient psalmist answers: it is the
commandments which make men wise, the testimonies which
give understanding (Ps. 119:98, 99). God's word is our
provision. Again this is not a matter of the intellect and
memory, as our Lord's engagement with Satan vividly
demonstrates. It is a matter of imbibing the teaching of
Scripture in the spirit of Scripture and with the fine balance of
Scripture *and* doing so in the context of a life of obedience to
and fellowship with God.

This is true particularly in the major 'problem' areas of
personal guidance — marriage and vocation. No amount of
teaching on guidance will show us whom to marry or what to
do with our lives. But it is precisely here that we find the
importance of knowing the Scriptures — for they teach us
basic structures and guidelines in both these areas, and it is
essentially the application of *these principles* which will help
us. Far more good can be done by a study of the biblical
doctrine of marriage, or gifts and vocation, than by impatient
waiting on a 'bolt from the blue'.

No one has encapsulated this better than John Newton:

> By treasuring up the doctrines, precepts, promises,
> examples and exhortations of Scripture, in their
> minds, and daily comparing themselves with the
> rule by which they walk, they grow into an
> habitual frame of spiritual wisdom, and acquire a
> gracious taste, which enables them to judge of right
> and wrong with a degree of readiness and
> certainty, as a musical ear judges of sounds. And
> they are seldom mistaken, because they are
> influenced by the love of Christ, which rules in
> their hearts, and a regard to the glory of God,
> which is the great object they have in view.
>
> *Works of John Newton* p. 88

This again is the viewpoint of Hebrews 5:12-14. We need to
have our senses trained by exercise in spiritual living to

discern the difference between good and evil, better and best. This is the difference between the child and the man; to be able to pierce through the clamour of the many voices which call us and entice us with their assurance of guidance, and distinguish the one sure way, mapped out in principle in Scripture, applied by the aid of the Holy Spirit in our own lives, and fully discovered as the good providence of God unfolds itself day by day before us.

The whole matter can be put another way. The hallmark of coming to know the will of God is *objectivity*. Jean Piaget, the French thinker and psychologist has suggested that the fundamental difference between childhood and truly adult thought is that while the child is dominated by an egocentric attitude to life and influenced by his own wishes and inner needs rather than the objective reality beyond him, the adult lives his life in the light of that world and brings his perception into line with it. It is surely obvious that there is a spiritual parallel. In the question of guidance, as in so many other areas, the basic need is for Christians to learn to be objective and in the best sense 'eccentric', that is to live their lives out of God as their centre rather than self as their centre; to escape from a self-dominated view of Christian living, and to see that their chief end is to glorify God, and enjoy *him*. It is the failure to do this that accounts for a great deal of our present confusion about guidance. When we are concerned to glorify God guidance will cease to be a *problem* and appear increasingly as a *joy and a privilege*. It is to this goal that all preaching and pastoral ministry is directed, until all Christians come to the stature of the fulness of Christ, and to mature manhood.

We can summarise this in the words of John Flavel:

> If therefore in doubtful cases, you would discover God's will, govern yourselves in your search after it by these rules.
> 1. Get the true fear of God upon your hearts: be really afraid of offending him; God will not hide his mind from such a soul (Ps. 25:14), 'The secret of the Lord is with them that fear him, and he will shew them his covenant.'
> 2. Study the *word* more, and the concerns and interests of the world less. The *word* is a light to your feet (Ps. 119:105) i.e. it hath a discovering and

directive usefulness as to all the duties to be done
and dangers to be avoided: It is the great oracle at
which you are to enquire. Treasure up its rules in
your hearts, and you will walk safely (Ps. 119:11),
'Thy word have I hid in my heart, that I might not
sin against thee.'

3. Reduce what you know into practice, and you
shall know what is your duty to practise (John
7:17), 'If any man do his will, he shall know of the
doctrine.' (Ps. 111:10), 'A good understanding have
all they that do his commandments.'

4. Pray for illumination and direction in the way
that you should go; beg the Lord to guide you in
straits, and that he would not suffer you to fall into
sin. This was the holy practice of Ezra 8:21. 'Then I
proclaimed a fast there at the river Ahava, that we
might afflict ourselves before our God, to seek of
him a right way for us, and for our little ones, and
for all of our substance.'

5. And this being done, follow providence so far as
it agrees with the word, and no further.

Works IV:470-471

This is but the standpoint of Psalm 37:

Trust in the Lord and do good; . . .
Delight yourself in the Lord
    and he will give you the
        desires [petitions] of your heart.
Commit your way to the Lord;
    trust in him and he will do
        this: . . .
Be still before the Lord [Be silent to the Lord] and
    wait patiently for him.

Facing difficulties

6

The problem of sin

When many of us became Christians we were given a series of
texts to memorise and to use as guide-posts in our Christian
life. Such texts are usually those which summarise in a few
words a good deal of biblical truth in a variety of areas. The
selection found on different cards or leaflets inevitably varies,
but there are a few texts which seem to appear constantly. In
previous chapters we have seen that growth in the Christian
life involves entering into many of the privileges which God
has provided for us; these 'memory-verses' consequently
include words on forgiveness, assurance, guidance,
consecration and obedience. They may also include some
biblical exhortation to be quit with sin, and to deal with it
whenever it comes to the surface in our lives. In that
connection there is no verse of the Bible more familiar than the
famous words of 'The Psalm of Maturity':

> How can a young man keep his way pure? By
> living according to your word.
>
> (Ps. 119:9)

We are turning back once again, therefore, to this ancient
psalm from which we have already derived spiritual wisdom,
to see what it has to teach us about dealing with sin in the
Christian life. Sin is the internal enemy of our development as
believers. It is the Fifth Column which has been established in
our hearts, and it is of fundamental importance that we are

aware of its presence and equally know how to stem its flow
and stay its baneful influences. That little word *how* is perhaps
the key to things. Yet many Christians never seem to use it as
an important part of their vocabulary.

The Question — How?
   God has given us an abundance of aids to bring us to
maturity. It is worth listing them:

The word of God
The ministry of the Holy Spirit
The ministry of preaching and teaching
The various ministries of the fellowship of Christians
The privilege of prayer
The circumstances of our lives — our calling, our experiences
The guidance of other Christians

But in each case we ought to ask the question — How? This
was what the writer of Psalm 119 realised so clearly. It is one
thing to be encouraged and commanded to a life of purity. But
how does it work out in daily living? Whenever we read a
passage which directs us to holiness; whenever we read a book
which challenges us to a new level of surrender to Christ;
whenever we listen to a message which makes us deeply
conscious of our need to deal with the sin which remains in our
lives, we must ask and go on asking this question — *How?*
   Psalm 119 is a very interesting part of Scripture. There are a
number of clues contained in it which indicate its origin and
purpose. For one thing, it is *an acrostic poem*. It is divided into
the same number of eight-verse sections as there are letters in
the Hebrew alphabet. In each section all the verses begin with
the same letter. These 176 verses were intended for
memorisation — and this was simply a device to aid the
memory. But the Psalm was also, as verse eight indicates,
written *for young men*. Not that its teaching excluded
application to old men, or young women either for that matter!
But it was a deeply-rooted facet of the spiritual education of the
young people of the Jewish church, to fit them for the service of
God in future generations. If a young man learned to keep his

way pure *as a young man* it augured well for his future. Gains
made in the heart in youth are the most important of all:

> Sow a thought, reap an act
> Sow an act, reap a character
> Sow a character, reap a destiny.

But clearly this is not merely a young man's question. At a
later stage in his life St Augustine once wrote, in the deep
consciousness of his continuing sinfulness: 'I have become a
puzzle to myself.' He was simply repeating the *cri de coeur* of
the apostle Paul 'Who can deliver me from this body of death?'
(Rom. 7:24). And there are times in every Christian's
experience when that kind of longing is wrung from our very
depths as we feel keenly the flesh warring against the
influences of the Spirit. Then this question inevitably arises —
How can we keep our way clean?

THE PERPLEXITY OF INDWELLING SIN

In fact this whole section of Pslam 119 provides us with the
answer to our question. But before examining the testimony of
an older teacher to God's help, we must first consider further
this spiritual perplexity, this heavy burden of sin. There is a
famous work of theology, written in the last years of the
eleventh century by a man called Anselm, entitled in Latin *Cur
Deus Homo*, Why God became Man. It is in the form of a
discussion between the author and someone who has been
questioning him about the meaning of Christ's incarnation and
death. At one point, Anselm replies to an objection in these
words: '*You have not yet paid attention to the greatness of the
weight of sin.*' Those words are just as true of our
understanding of the Christian life as they are of
understanding the death of Jesus. It is a fundamental mistake
to treat sin lightly, or not to be conscious of its presence and
power in our own Christian lives. No one has written more
forcefully or clearly about this than the famous nineteenth
century Anglican Bishop, J.C. Ryle:

> He that wishes to attain right views about
> Christian holiness, must begin by examining the
> vast and solemn subject of sin. He must dig down
> very low if he would build high. A mistake here is
> most mischievous. Wrong views about holiness
> are generally traceable to wrong views about
> human corruption ...
> The plain truth is that a right knowledge of sin lies
> at the root of all saving Christianity. Without it
> such doctrines as justification, conversion,
> sanctification, are 'words and names' which
> convey no meaning to the mind.
>
> *Holiness* p.1

This is precisely the concern expressed in Psalm 119:8. You
will see that most clearly by reading the verse out to yourself. It
is possible to emphasise virtually every word in it, and find a
fresh shade of significance in the question by doing so:

How can a young man keep his way pure?
How **can** a young man keep his way pure?
How can **a young** man keep his way pure?
How can a young **man** keep his way pure?
How can a young man **keep** his way pure?
How can a young man keep **his way** pure?
How can a young man keep his way **pure?**

Long custom and use has led us to understand these words
in the following way:

Question: How can a young man keep his way pure?
Answer: By living according to God's word.

There is certainly a good deal of truth in that answer, as we
shall see. *But it is not in fact what the psalmist appears to have
written.* For the original may be read: How can a young man
keep his way pure *in order to* guard it according to God's
word? In other words, the word of God is not so much the
answer to his problem but part of the cause of it. That may
seem a very startling, even mistaken, thing to say. How can
God's word which calls us to holiness, obedience and purity, be
the cause of this common problem? But to ask the question is to
begin to answer it. For it is because the Bible calls us to holiness

of life and tells us that without it we will never see the Lord
(Heb. 12:14) that we have this problem at all. The Psalms
themselves are full of illustrations of men who have no regard
for God or his word and for whom holiness and purity are
neither problems nor burdens. You live your own life in regular
contact with similar men. What makes you stand out as a
Christian is that one of the concerns you have is the longing to
be purer, cleaner and more like your Lord Jesus Christ.

Now, naturally, this is not the whole truth. But it is the truth
which these famous words enshrine and if we understand
them aright we cannot fail to profit from them. After all, the
psalmist is only being true to experience. We have already
noted how burdened the apostle Paul was after he became a
Christian about his own sinfulness. It is not uncommon to hear
people say that they have come to a deeper sense of their own
sinfulness since they became Christians than they did while
they were being drawn to Christ. This is simply the
continuation and maturation of the work of God's Holy Spirit
within us, convicting us of sin in order that we may direct our
hearts increasingly to the forgiveness and peace which is ours
in Christ.

John Bunyan captures the meaning behind Psalm 119:8 in a
very wonderful way in *The Pilgrim's Progress*. Early on in the
book he pictures Christian heeding the instructions of
Evangelist to go to the wicket gate and make his way to the
Cross if he would be freed from the burden he is carrying. That
burden is his own sinfulness. But soon he meets up with Mr
Worldly Wiseman:

> Master Worldly Wiseman therefore having some
> guess of him, by beholding his laborious going, by
> observing his sighs and groans, and the like; began
> thus to enter into some talk with Christian.
>
> *Worldly Wiseman*: How now, good fellow, whither
> away after this burdened manner?
> *Christian*: A burdened manner indeed, as ever, I
> think, poor creature had! And whereas you ask me,
> 'Whither away?' I tell you, sir, I am going to yonder
> Wicket Gate before me; for there, as I am informed,
> I shall be put into a Way to be rid of my heavy
> Burden.

Worldly Wiseman: Hast thou a wife and children?

Christian: Yes; but I am so laden with this burden, that I cannot take pleasure in them as formerly: me thinks, I am as if I had none.

Worldly Wiseman: Wilt thou hearken to me if I give thee counsel?

Christian: If it be good, I will; for I stand in need of good counsel.

Worldly Wiseman: I would advise thee then, that thou with all speed get thyself rid of thy burden; for thou wilt never be settled in thy mind till then. Nor canst thou enjoy the benefits of the blessings which God hath bestowed upon thee, till then.

Christian: That is that which I seek for, even to be rid of this heavy burden; but get it off myself, I cannot. Nor is there a man in our country that can take it off my shoulders; therefore am I going this way, as I told you, that I may be rid of my burden.

Worldly Wiseman: Who bid thee go this way to be rid of thy burden?

Christian: A man that appeared to me to be a very great and honourable person; his name, as I remember, is Evangelist.

Worldly Wiseman: Beshrew him for his counsel, there is not a more dangerous and troublesome way in the world, than is that unto which he hath directed thee; and that thou shalt find, if thou wilt be ruled by his counsel. Thou hast met with something (as I perceive) already; for I see the dirt of the Slough of Despond is upon thee; but that slough is the beginning of the sorrows that do attend those that go on in that Way. Hear me, I am older than thou; thou art like to meet with, in the way which thou goest, Wearisomeness, Painfulness, Hunger, Perils, Nakedness, Sword, Lions, Dragons, Darkness, and in a word, Death, and what not? These things are certainly true, having been confirmed by many testimonies. And why should a man so carelessly cast away himself, by giving heed to a stranger?

Christian: Why, sir, this burden upon my back is more terrible to me than are all these things which you have mentioned. Nay, methinks I care not what I meet with in the way, if so be I can also meet with deliverance from my Burden.

Worldly Wiseman: How camest thou by thy burden at first?

Christian: BY READING THIS BOOK IN MY HAND.

The book to which Christian referred was the Bible. Reading
it, discovering what it had to say about the nature of God and
the nature of sin; about the grace of God and the rebellion of
man; looking into it like a mirror in which his own character
was graphically illustrated — he could not fail to be burdened
and perplexed by his own failure before God. It is not
surprising that he rebukes the tempting Wiseman with the
words 'I know what I would obtain; it is ease for my heavy
burden'. He was thinking particularly of the guilt of his sin, and
the burden which would soon roll from him as he eventually
disregarded the advice given to him and made his way with the
help of Evangelist to the Cross where his burden rolled away.
But the pattern of his experience is often repeated later in the
Christian's pilgrimage, when he learns enough about himself to
realise that he has so much further to go in his search for
holiness. It is not for nothing we learn to sing that:

> Hindrances strew all the way
> I aim at thee, yet from thee stray.

It is worth noting that in Psalm 119 at least the burden of
indwelling sin is made all the heavier by a number of extra
difficulties.

(a) **The Opposition of others.** Throughout the psalm this is a
recurring theme (see verses 51, 61, 69, 78, 85, 110 particularly).
Sometimes the opposition is obvious: 'The arrogant mock me
without restraint' (v.51), 'The arrogant have smeared me with
lies' (v.69). Sometimes the approach is much more subtle and
the opposition unseen — 'The arrogant dig pitfalls for me'
(v.85), 'The wicked have set a snare for me' (v.110) — when the
opposition disguises itself in some other, possibly more
tempting or more plausible way. It takes many young
Christians or older Christians in new situations some time
before they have the measure of the difficulties they face and
are able by the testimony of their lives to silence the degrading
comments of others round about them. That can prove to be a
difficult experience and all the more so when we have become
conscious of our own very real weaknesses.

We certainly are in great need today of recognising that there is opposition throughout our society, indeed throughout the whole of our civilisation, to the holiness which the Christian will want to exhibit. A document which is alleged to have come into the possession of a Field Director of the American Security Council in the 1960s illustrates this in an almost prophetic way. Entitled 'Revolution by Stealth' it listed the objectives of atheistic communism in western civilisation which could be achieved without resort to arms. Some of these were as follows:

> Break down cultural standards of morality by promoting pornography and obscenity in books, magazines, motion pictures, radio and TV.
> Eliminate all laws governing obscenity by calling them 'censorship' and 'a violation of free speech and free press'.
> Discredit the family as an institution. Encourage promiscuity and easy divorce.
> Gain control of key positions in radio, TV and motion pictures.
> Present homosexuality, degeneracy, and promiscuity as 'normal, natural and healthy'.

And so the list goes on. A book like Mary Whitehouse's *Whatever Happened to Sex?* indicates the extent to which these aims, whether deliberately or accidentally, have been fulfilled in our present Western Society. The Christian has a God-given duty to do something about the situation. But his *first* duty is not to complain, or even to exercise his democratic right as a citizen to call for a 'clean-up'. No, his first duty is to recognise that Christians, particularly younger ones, live in a society which operates according to a different set of moral rules from the one which existed a few decades ago — and the pressures to conform *and therefore* the opposition there is to Christian holiness has correspondingly increased. If we do not recognise that the moral sickness of the society around us adds to our personal burden to be distinctive in purity, then we have already fallen prey to the 'snare' which has been dug for us (Ps. 119:110).

(b) **The evils of his own heart.** The psalmist speaks about the possibility of 'wandering' from God's commandments (v.10). He has clearly made an important discovery about himself — that he has this native tendency to drift away from full and joyful obedience to the word of God. That is a very disturbing thing to know about ourselves, but for many Christians it is an essential step to going further in spiritual living. In verse 37 he prays 'Turn my eyes away from worthless things', because he had become aware of his perverse ability to drift almost unconsciously, and then uncontrollably to gaze on the empty pleasures of the world. Our media-ridden society provides even more opportunity for this than primitive Palestine did. We need to be alert to these temptations and also to the fact that the wandering eye is not unconnected to the wandering heart.

It is doubtful whether we take these issues as seriously as we should. It was the saintly Robert Murray M'Cheyne who once wrote in his diary that he had now come to realise that the seed of every known sin was present in his heart. How easy to treat such a statement lightly without realising that by doing so we are guilty of repressing a basic truth about ourselves too. Our hearts are not only naturally 'desperately wicked' says Jeremiah, but they are also 'deceitful' (Jer. 17:9). The word he uses means 'slippery', 'difficult to hold firm'. How accurate a picture that is! As soon as there is any depth of conviction of sin our hearts wriggle out of being nailed down by God's Spirit into confession, cleansing and fresh empowering, and consecration to true holiness. Instead they slip away from the Spirit's grasp and we refuse to allow the Lord to get to the very bottom of our lives to thoroughly cleanse and forgive us. It is because of this that the Bible warns us about the danger of the deceitfulness of sin and advises us to 'be not deceived'. Here in Psalm 119 we have one testimony to the experience of being 'undeceived' by God's word. When that happens we can no longer regard the Christian life as something we live casually. It must be lived seriously or not at all. We cannot continue *disguising* sin; nor will we be satisfied by *diverting* sin, when the fear of discovery makes us channel our secret wanderings into some less-obvious, less-frowned-upon form of self indulgence and breach of God's law. On the contrary, it is a mark of grace to allow ourselves to be exposed before God, to hide nothing from him, and to be conscious of our native wanderings to the point of being sickened by our own failure, and long for a clean heart and a new spirit (Ps. 51:10).

THE KEY TO THE SITUATION

If the word of God is not in fact part of the answer the psalmist gives to his perplexity — at least, in this verse — how are we to understand the way forward? How did he come to keep his way pure? He suggests three lines of action.

(a) **He began to seek God**. 'I seek you with all my heart; do not let me stray from your commands' he writes in verse 10. Of course he is not thinking here of the philosopher's search for God, analysing the arguments for his existence and reviewing the many objections brought against them. For this man the existence of God was not the result of an argument, but the foundation of any possible intellectual pursuit. He presupposed, believed, and was certain of, the existence of God. God was there. That was not his difficulty. His problem was that while God was there, he was here — in a world of sin, and with a heart at an infinite distance from God's holiness. What he lacked was not intellectual conviction, but spiritual inclination. This was the message of Isaiah, in the great evangelistic passage towards the end of his prophecy: 'Seek the Lord while he may be found; call on him while he is near' — that is the way to find yourself in God's presence; 'Let the wicked forsake his way and the evil man his thoughts' — that is the cost of discovering his presence; 'Let him turn to the Lord, and he will have mercy on him, and to our God, for he will freely pardon' — that is the chief blessing of being in his presence.

When this search took place an unexpected lesson was learned. He was a sinner seeking a holy God. He came in fear and trembling. But no sooner is he in the presence of God than we find him quite unselfconsciously expressing deep praise and adoration, 'Praise be to you, O Lord' (v.12); 'Blessed art

thou, O Lord', as other translations express it. He had sought
the *Holy One* of Israel, and found the *Blessed One*. That is the
surprise which is experienced only by the wholehearted: 'I seek
you with all my heart' he had said (v.10), and so he received the
fulfilment of God's promise through Jeremiah: 'You will seek
me and find me when you seek me with all your heart' (Jer.
29:13). People who do anything whole-heartedly usually find
an exhileration which is unknown to the half-hearted, whether
it be in the sphere of work, or play, or human relationships. Our
consciousness of sin within mars our joy in our supreme
relationship. If we would have it restored we must be
wholehearted in our return to God.

(b) **He began to treasure God's word.** How marvellous to see
that God's word not only places the burden of holiness on our
shoulders but enables us to lift it. There is a sanctifying power
in the word of God so that our Lord could pray: 'make them
holy through your truth; your word is the truth' (John 17:17).

Today we have a marked tendency to think of this in terms
of personal Bible reading, and at first sight the famous words
of Psalm 119:11 lend weight to that: 'I have hidden your word
in my heart that I might not sin against you.' But it is in fact
more likely, throughout Scripture, that references like these are
inclusive of the public explanation and application of God's
word which is associated with a preaching ministry. It cannot
be stressed too highly just how fundamental this principle is to
our lives. Later on in the psalm, he parallels 'Direct my
footsteps according to your word' with 'let no sin rule over me'
(Ps. 119:133). He is praying in part for God's word itself to
deliver him from the dominion of sin in his life. What a
marvellous thing it is to see this accomplished through
preaching. We come to a service conscious of defeat and failure;
we have prayed, striven, read Scripture, consulted books, but
we seem to have made so little real progress and our sin weighs
us down like a heavy burden. Then we find that God
wonderfully sends out shafts of light into our hearts, and the
sword of the Spirit not only exposes our sin but cuts us loose
from its fetters. The hymn writer Charitie Lees De Chenez puts
the experience in these words:

The King of Glory standeth
Beside that heart of sin;
His mighty voice commandeth
The raging waves within;
The floods of deepest anguish
Roll backward at his will
As o'er the storm ariseth
His mandate, 'Peace be still'.

At times, with sudden glory,
He speaks, and all is done;
Without one stroke of battle
The victory is won,
While we, with joy beholding,
Can scarce believe it true
That even our kingly Jesus
Can form such hearts anew.

In the presence of true preaching the mind is wonderfully concentrated by the Spirit, a searching and exposing takes place within our hearts; our deadened affections are awakened into newness of life and we know the powerful influence of God's word which is able to deliver us from sin and uncleanness.

(c) **He began to rejoice in God's way of salvation**. In verse 14 he writes: 'I rejoice in following your statutes as one rejoices in great riches.' The 'statutes' of God are not so much his commands but the principles by which he governs our lives and provides for our spiritual well-being. They include the declarations of what he has done and will do for the full salvation of his people. In this the psalmist rejoices. Did he not lead God's people out of the bondage of Egypt? Has he not given to them the message of forgiveness and salvation? Then the psalmist will yield himself to God, his promises, his ways, and the means he has provided for spiritual growth.

For the Christian, living in the full blaze of the revelation of the New Testament this has special significance. For the testimony of God to him is found in the Cross of Christ. There lies the deliverance of God from sin; and he knows that he cannot embrace that cross, or, more important, embrace the Christ who died on it and now lives for ever in the service of God, without renouncing all known sin. We cannot serve two masters — a crucified Christ who died for our sin, and sin for which he died. The more we rejoice in the way of salvation, therefore, the more we will mortify sin. That will not make us perfect, because there is no complete mortification in this life. But it will bring us joy in walking in the power of Christ and being delivered from the power of sin. This, in part, is the answer to our common perplexity: How can we keep our way pure?

7

Overcoming temptation

We have found that going on to Christian maturity is a morally demanding matter. Growing in grace contains a number of surprises, and one is the *new conflicts* which appear in Christian experience. It is not unusual to meet young Christians who expected something quite different in the Christian life from what they discovered. Instead — as the Bible indicates in a variety of ways — not only are dimensions of blessing opened up which they never imagined existed, but dimensions of evil, outside and within, come to the surface and have to be reckoned with.

It is in this context that we must now consider the subject of *temptation.* Tertullian, one of the early Christian theologians, who lived during the last half of the second and first quarter of the third centuries, tells us that Jesus once said: 'No one can obtain the kingdom of heaven who has not passed through temptation.' Of course we have no way of verifying whether Jesus ever said this or not. But there can be no doubt that the saying itself is true, for temptation is part and parcel of every Christian's experience. If we entertained any doubts about that they are dispelled for us by the Lord's Prayer, which is really a marvellous summary of the Christian life and the ways in which we need God's grace to live it. There we are taught our *daily* need to pray for protection from temptation. That petition has a unique importance and we must consider it with some care later. For the moment it is worth examining what the

Bible means by the expressions 'tempt' and 'temptation' in order to see how this sometimes painful experience fits in to God's purposes to bring his children to maturity.

Two very important principles must first of all be enunciated.

1. In the Bible, 'to tempt' carries the suggestion of *putting to the test* rather than inciting to sin. Naturally, in the test such incitement may be present, but it is not normally the primary element.

2. In biblical teaching *temptation is not sin*. That is a principle of enormous practical importance. Many sincere Christians have been paralysed by Satan precisely here, and made to feel that simply because they have been tempted to a particular sin, they have already sinned and come under the displeasure of God. It is vital therefore to see the distinction between temptation and sin. It may help us if we remind ourselves that Jesus was tempted (Heb. 4:15). Yet he was *without sin* and therefore to suggest that temptation is a sin is to come close to blasphemy — and there are occasions when a strong reminder like that will clarify the minds which Satan has confused.

How then can we distinguish temptation from sin when both seem to cling closely to us? *By asking ourselves whether we want the temptation which is set before us.* If our hearts are set against it, then we may be sure that we are *not* yet engaged in sin but *are* being subjected to temptation.

In fact the Bible has two different sets of words for temptation in the Hebrew of the Old Testament and the Greek of the New Testament. One conveys the idea of testing in order to prove validity. In the word-picture of Scripture, the believer is tested for genuineness just as metal is tested for its genuineness. The other word normally has a less positive content, and conveys more the idea of testing through temptation, through the experience of the opportunity to sin. The first expression is *never* used of Satan, the second is *infrequently* used of God. But when God does test, it is in order to know what is in the hearts of men and women. He applies pressure on their lives to see what will emerge. This is a regular theme in the Old Testament (Deut. 8:2; Judges 2:22; 3: 1-4; 2 Chron. 32:31).

LED INTO TEMPTATION

As we suggested earlier, however, there is a further dimension
to the experience of temptation. We are taught to pray
regularly, 'Lead us not into temptation, but deliver us from
evil'. Perhaps of all the petitions of the Lord's Prayer this one
has given the greatest perplexity, and consequently many
writers have prefaced their exposition of it by indicating that
while God may *test us* (Gen. 22:1ff.), he never *tempts* us in the
sense of soliciting us to sin, as this petition might seem to
suggest.

It is a pity if our understanding goes no further than that. For
while it may be true and necessary to stress this point, it is not
really an explanation of our Lord's words. Nor do those words,
properly considered, really suggest that God solicits us to sin.
What they do presuppose is that he will sometimes *lead* us into
temptation. He who takes the flock beside still waters and
through green pastures into the paths of righteousness may
also direct them to the valley of deep darkness and temptation.
It is this possibility which is to shape the prayer we make for
protection and deliverance. No doubt Christ's own experience
lay at the back of his mind as he taught the disciples these
words, for only recently he had been '*led* by the Spirit into the
desert *to be tempted* by the devil' (Matt. 4:1). God did not tempt
him, nor solicit him to sin, but the Scripture makes plain that
God was involved, by the Spirit, in leading Christ into
temptation. We must therefore agree with the principle laid
down by John Owen when he wrote: 'It is true that God *tempts
none*, as temptation formally leads unto sin; but he *orders
temptations*.'

What is involved in being led into temptation? Again the
example of Christ's life teaches us that it means more than
ordinary temptation, for his whole life is described as the time
of his temptations (Luke 22:28). There is something distinctive
about being *led* into temptation.

We are led into temptation and enter into it (Matt. 26:41)
when the three chief avenues of temptation are opened
concurrently and pressure is exerted on the soul through their
combined force. Thus a man may be tempted when he is lured
and enticed by the *flesh* (Jas. 1:14); but when these desires are

further stimulated by the *world* and aggravated by the work of the *devil* then he has entered into temptation. Being led *into* temptation therefore means the concentration and persistence of enticement to sin. Thus John Calvin understands the petition and writes, 'Here is intended that interior temptation which may aptly be termed the devil's lash, for whipping up our concupiscence', and Owen again shrewdly comments, 'Whilst it knocks at the door we are at liberty; but when any temptation comes in and parleys with the heart, reasons with the mind, entices and allures the affections, be it a longer or shorter time, do it thus insensibly and imperceptibly, or do the soul take notice of it, we "enter into temptation".' Natural disposition of temperament or the restraints of society may still preserve us if only one of temptation's avenues is open. But when we discover that our awakened desire for sin is given free opportunity to exercise itself and every encouragement to do so, then the grace of God alone is sufficient preservative; the 'evil day' (Eph. 6:13) has come, temptation has reached its height and *deliverance* has become the need of the hour if we are to remain standing when the battle is done.

The very nature of being led into temptation should be sufficient encouragement to us to pray for protection and deliverance. But how unconscious Christians can be of their own weakness and of the tempter's power! Thomas Boston, a great Scottish preacher of a bygone age, put it with startling power when he said that Satan 'has now had several thousand years experience in the hellish trade. He has his devices for trapping poor mortals, and knows how to suit his temptations, as they may best take'. He has successfully campaigned since the beginning of time and the history of the world bears eloquent testimony to the shipwrecks he has caused in the whirlpools of temptation. This is surely why our Lord encouraged this daily necessity of prayer for personal and corporate deliverance.

THE PATTERN OF TEMPTATION

How does temptation work? The pages of Scripture abound with examples of the nature of temptation, but perhaps none is more vivid and illuminating than the experience of King David recorded in 2 Samuel 11-12 and Psalm 51. Here we find the unfolding of temptation's *occasion, progress* and *harvest*.

(a) **The occasion of temptation** was *a time of unprecedented success* and blessing in David's life. He had seen the power of God and experienced his faithfulness; a long cherished ambition to bring the Ark of the Covenant to Jerusalem had been fulfilled, and the altercation he had with Michal on that day (2 Sam. 6:21-23) revealed the measure to which he had died to the adulations of the world, and the degree to which he was rejoicing in the privileges of God's choice of him and finding comfort in it. The past decade had been one of advance and prosperity. But in the midst of this blessing evil lay close at hand and soon did its deceptive work. David had apparently not learned from the examples of his forefathers that times of spiritual prosperity draw Satan to the believer's side.

Temptation came too at *a time of neglected duty*. It was 'at the time when kings go off to war' (2 Sam. 11:1). But David lay on his couch! What a tragic figure, clothed in the leisure wear of his own self-indulgence instead of the armour of God's king! It is no surprise to discover that having neglected his public duty as king of Israel he was soon to neglect his personal duty as a man of God, for failure to be about our duties inevitably leads to greater temptations being met by weaker resistance. It leads to a paralysis by the devil. What timely instruction this always is. It ought never to be forgotten that the purpose of God's grace in our hearts is not to *excuse* duty, but to *promote* it: 'It teaches us to say "No" to ungodliness and worldly passions, and to live self-controlled, upright and godly lives in this present age' (Titus 2:11, 12). The Christian's duties therefore are prescribed by God in his word, and not by his own natural disposition and personal interests. Only when he follows Scripture and applies it to himself will he be safe from sin. Again we find help in some of the old masters of the spiritual life at this point. Thomas Brooks wrote in his valuable book, with the striking title, *Precious Remedies Against Satan's Devices*: 'If you would not be taken by any of Satan's devices then walk by rule. He that walks by rule walks most safely; he that walks by rule walks most honourably; he that walks by rule walks most sweetly.'

If we love Christ we will keep his commandments (John 14:15). Perhaps there is no greater cause of sin and spiritual decline in many lives than this simple one. Let us be at our duties.

(b) **The progress of temptation** develops through different stages — aggravation, deception and captivation. This again is pressed home to us in the case of David. His fall is traced in 2 Samuel 11:2-4 by the use of seven main verbs, representing the inexorable progress of unchallenged temptation as it works towards its goal of sin and death. It works by *aggravation* — the pleasures of sin for a season were a small price for the devil to pay for the ruin of David's testimony. It works by *deception* — it was never David's intention to go so far as adultery and murder, nor to lose his fellowship with God. But temptation also works by *captivation*, and without so much as drawing the sword of the Spirit from its sheath with its 'Thou shalt not commit adultery' and 'Thou shalt not kill', David took the first step of adultery (2 Sam. 11:4) and soon discovered that more transgression was demanded to pay the price of a conscience blackmailed by the evil one. And so he was responsible soon for murder (2 Sam. 11:14ff.). Perhaps James had this sad tale with its miserable conclusion in mind when he wrote of the progress of temptation: 'Each one is tempted when, by his own evil desire, he is dragged away and enticed. Then, after desire has conceived, it gives birth to sin; and sin, when it is full-grown, gives birth to death' (Jas. 1:14, 15).

> Sin rather than 'twill out of action be
> Will pray to stay, though but a while with thee,
> One night, one hour, one moment, will it cry,
> Embrace me in thy bosom else I die:
> Time to repent (saith it) I will allow,
> And help, if to repent thou knowest not how.
> But if you give it entrance at the door
> It will come in, and may go out no more.
> John Bunyan

(c) So David reaped the inevitable **harvest of temptation**. Not simply in the physical death of the child that was born (2 Sam. 12:18), but in the judgment on his life which that symbolised. Something in David died, and though he was graciously restored it would still be true to say that in terms of his usefulness to the kingdom of God his life was never really the same again. In the short term he knew nine months of separation from God until his conscience was alarmed under Nathan's ministry (2 Sam. 12:14), and in the long term he experienced a lifetime of recurring shame. So he writes in Psalm 51 of a heart that was polluted (v.2) and of a conscience that was wounded (v.3); of a sense of the judgment of God (v.4); of a loss of spiritual joy (v.8), of assurance (v.11) and all the privileges of adoption (v.12).

This Scriptural record is a lamp to our feet and a light to our path — it *reveals* what the tempter *conceals*. Since the beginning he has held out life. But from before the beginning God has revealed the tempter's way to be death. If we know our weaknesses, we will want to pray for protection:

> Prone to wander, Lord I feel it
> Prone to leave the God I love
> Take my heart, O take and seal it
> Seal it for thy courts above.
> Robert Robinson

THE PURPOSE OF TEMPTATION

But this raises the fundamental question: why should God lead us into temptation? Martin Luther provided one answer: 'Unus Christianus temptatus mille' — 'One Christian who has been tempted is worth a thousand who haven't.' For God does a work in his children through temptation that he does in no other way. In his hands it is a means, not of destruction, but of sanctification. That is why, though the Christian may experience great heaviness in his manifold temptations he is still able to rejoice (1 Pet. 1:6).

God may lead us into temptation *to chasten us for sin*. This is part of the meaning of those strange Old Testament passages in which both God and Satan are attributed with leading David into the sin of numbering Israel (1 Sam. 24:1ff.; 1 Chron.

21:1ff.). It was because 'The anger of the Lord was kindled against Israel' that David was thus led by God to be tempted by the devil. That experience brought fresh depths of repentance and new supplies of grace to David's life. The same is true at a more personal level of Simon Peter. Satan had demanded to have him to sift him like wheat (Luke 22:31) and God had acceded to the demand. But through his temptation and failure Peter remembered the word of the Lord (Matt. 26:75); his heart was broken and emptied of its former pride and self-reliance. Thus chastised he became subject to the Father of spirits and lived (Heb. 12:9f.). Such an experience, to borrow an illustration from John Owen, is like the barks of the sheepdog that the shepherd has sent after an erring sheep. They make it ready to hear the shepherd's voice. Thus tempted, the child of God discovers what he really is, and learns to think less of himself and more of his Saviour. So Job confessed 'I abhor myself and repent in dust and ashes' (Job 42:6). So when David was brought up out of the pit into which his soul had fallen, the *new* song in his mouth was 'praise to our God' (Ps. 40:2, 3).

God may also lead us into temptation *to make us more like Christ.* That is his purpose in all things (Rom. 8:29). The early Christians used to say: 'He was made like us in order to be tempted. We are tempted in order to be made like him.' As the husbandman prunes the branches of the vine that they may bear more fruit, so the Father leads us into temptation to purge away everything that inhibits communion with Christ. He thus polishes our graces, matures our faith and increases our assurance. It is surely no accident that the Bible's symbol for joy is the wine that comes from *crushed* grapes for there is a sense in which the sweetest graces are sometimes only crushed out of the believer. The real importance of knowing that *God* may lead us into temptations is therefore the encouragement that knowledge gives to us to look for his hand and purpose in the midst of them.

DELIVERANCE

In what ways then does God 'deliver us from evil'? He *can* deliver the godly out of temptation (2 Pet. 2:9) and he does so in two ways. He sometimes delivers us by *sovereign intervention.* He has promised to keep us from all evil (Ps. 121:7), and to do so he will restrain the powers of darkness so that we will not be tempted beyond our strength (1 Cor. 10:13). He may remove our sinful desires when temptation is at its height, or alter our circumstances so that the object of temptation is removed from us. In heaven we will marvel that he who keeps Israel has neither slumbered nor slept (Ps. 121:3, 4), and in that sense Robert Murray M'Cheyne's words are particularly true:

> Then, Lord, shall I fully know,
> Not till then, how much I owe.

But God's secret and sovereign ways are not the *rule* which guides our conduct. That rule is his word, and ordinarily he delivers us from evil by the *spiritual provision* he offers to us through the Scriptures. The word 'deliver' has the basic meaning of drawing to oneself for safety and security. In keeping with this the means by which God delivers us from evil are those which bring us within the sphere of his gracious influences. They can be logically deduced from the very nature of temptation, but Scripture highlights them by three exhortations:

Be armed. Here is the Christian's *defence* against the tempter. In Paul's teaching about the armour of God, the emphasis is on the *truth* of saving grace which protects us from the wiles of the devil. We are not ignorant of his devices, and we are familiar with defence strategy. We therefore share the confidence of Psalm 91, 'His truth shall be thy shield and buckler. Thou shalt not be afraid for the terror by night; nor for the arrow that flieth by day' (vv.4, 5).

Be watchful. Here is the Christian's *attitude* to the tempter. The New Testament uses three different words to express this, which may roughly be distinguished by the expressions — *Wake up!* (Matt. 24:42, 43; 1 Cor. 16:13; 1 Thess. 5:6; Rev. 3:2); *Stay awake!* (2 Tim. 4:5; 1 Pet. 4:7) and *Watch out!* (Mark 13:33; Luke 21:36; Eph. 6:18). These advise us of different aspects of spiritual watchfulness. We must be aware of the nature and power of temptation and of the influence of the tempter; we must know something about ourselves and our own special weaknesses in temptation; we must be trained to detect the presence of the enemy. The linguistic root of the word 'Satan' conveys the idea of 'one lying in ambush'. It suggests the hiddenness of his workings, the concealment of his identity. Therefore only constant vigilance will expose the identity of the foe, and bring spiritual deliverance.

Be prayerful. Here is the Christian's *weapon* against the tempter. We are to 'watch and *pray*' (Matt. 26:41); to 'be alert and always keep on praying' (Eph. 6:18). For prayer is approach to God through Christ and it is our heart-trust in Christ which ultimately drives Satan from us. So John Bunyan pictured the experience of Pilgrim as he made his way through the Valley of the Shadow:

> About the midst of this Valley, I perceived the mouth of Hell to be, and it stood also hard by the wayside: Now, thought Christian, what shall I do? And ever and anon the flame and smoke would come out in such abundance, with sparks and hideous noises, (things that cared not for Christian's sword, as did Apollyon before) that he was forced to put up his sword, and betake himself to another weapon called *All Prayer*: So he cried in my hearing, O Lord, I beseech thee, deliver my Soul ... Fiends seemed to come nearer and nearer: But when they were come even almost at him, he cried out with a most vehement voice, *I will walk in the strength of the Lord God*. So they gave back, and came no further.

The Lord has promised to hear those he has taught to pray. He will not turn a deaf ear to our cries for help. Yet the dependence thus produced in our hearts, as we later discover, is another sign that even through temptations he brings us *on to maturity*.

What then do we learn? We discover that we cannot avoid temptations of many kinds; we may even be led into them. But with the temptation, God 'will also provide a way out so that you can stand up under it' (1 Cor. 10:13). To thus remain standing, as the next chapter will show, is itself to advance in Christian maturity.

8

Fighting the enemy

We have already noted the importance of the prayer of
Epaphras, the pastor of the church at Colosse, that his people
might *stand* 'mature and fully assured' in all the will of God
(Col. 4:12). Already we have considered some of the elements
of the biblical teaching on assurance and guidance. But it is
important to notice that Paul's words suggest neither of these
blessings in itself is to be equated with Christian maturity. He
says that the burden of his friend's prayer was that Christians
might *stand* in their maturity. The ability to stand is of the
essence of Christian growth, just as it is of natural growth; the
baby crawls, then walks a few steps, but it takes a further
development to be able to stand firmly and surely for any
length of time.

In the New Testament the idea of standing has a quite
definite meaning. The thing that stands does not waver or
decay. It stays firm, whatever opposition may arise against it.
The sign of the mature Christian is not that he is able to run the
Christian race, but that he does so 'with perseverance' (Heb.
12:1); not that he is able to begin the battle for Christ, but that in
the battle he is able to remain standing. This is the central
theme of the well-known passage in Ephesians 6:10-20, and in
this chapter we will devote our attention to understanding its
relevance for Christian development.

The fundamental reason for considering Christian warfare
in a study of Christian progress is because the Bible underlines

the fact that while every believer enjoys the ministry of the Spirit as his *Helper* he also has to conflict with Satan as the *Hinderer*. Indwelling sin in the believer contends with the desires which the Spirit plants within him. That is a deep-seated and painful conflict; but it is exacerbated by the fact that it creates a perfect landing place for Satan. Paul speaks on several occasions of the work of grace being hindered, and in each case he evidently has an eye to the Hinderer (Gal. 5:7; Rom. 15:22; 1 Thess. 2:18). In the light of this, he has two things to say about the way to maturity through engaging against the forces of darkness.

THE CONFLICT IN WHICH WE ARE ENGAGED

> Finally, be strong in the Lord and in his mighty power. Put on the full armour of God so that you can take your stand against the devil's schemes. For our struggle is not against flesh and blood, but against the rulers, against the authorities, against the powers of this dark world and against the spiritual forces of evil in the heavenly realms. Therefore put on the full armour of God, so that when the day of evil comes, you may be able to stand your ground, and after you have done everything, to stand.
>
> (Eph. 6:10-13)

(a) It is very easy to miss *the context in which Paul wrote* these words. Of course it is true that we engage in conflict with the devil at many levels of our Christian experience and particularly in the work of evangelism when our concern is for the opening of the eyes of those whom Satan has blinded to the gospel lest they believe it (2 Cor. 4:4). But the context which gave rise to this teaching in Paul's own mind was a discussion of the various duties which the gospel creates for Christians in different roles in society. In the verses immediately preceding he had been discussing the relationships between husbands and wives, parents and children, masters and servants. It should not surprise us that he did so, for a moment's reflection makes us realise that all our service for Christ can be minimised in its usefulness if we can be tripped up or hindered in these basic relationships.

Simon Peter tells husbands to treat their wives with respect 'so that nothing will hinder your prayers' (1 Pet. 3:7), and the opening pages of the Bible tell us how that work of hindering developed first of all within the context of the home and led to the friction and division which was the forerunner of so much later unhappiness, with accusation and counter-accusation flying between husband and wife. How easily a young Christian's witness is marred and nullified because he is not the son, the brother, the worker that God has called him to be! How subtle Satan is, so that Paul finds it necessary to expose him in this routine area of life.

But that is not the only important thing he says about the context of this conflict. He further suggests that it is not flesh and blood we contend with but powers 'in the heavenly realms' (v.12). That phrase has a familiar ring about it to the reader of Ephesians. God has already blessed us in Christ, says Paul in 1:3, 'in the heavenly realms'; he has raised us up with Christ to sit 'in the heavenly realms in Christ Jesus', he says in 2:6. God wants to show in the church the multi-coloured glory of Christ to the authorities 'in the heavenly realms' (3:10). This, then, is a very important thing to grasp. The arena of blessing in the Christian life, the realm where we are united to Christ and share in heavenly blessing, actually introduces us to where the conflict between God and Satan is fiercest. That is true in many ways. Those fundamental relationships we have with one another in society, which Paul had just mentioned, are really the greatest blessings we can know — home, family and daily work. But precisely there Satan strives to undermine the goodness of God. Then, we find that it is on the crest of the wave of spiritual blessings and advance that Satan comes. We rightly think that it is often after special blessing that he comes. But the perspective of the New Testament is also that in order to receive spiritual blessing we must be drawn up into Christ — and it is right there that the attack of Satan is directed.

Awareness of Satan's plans is half the battle, and 'we are not unaware of his schemes' (2 Cor. 2:11).

(b) But we not only need to be aware of *the context* in which we are to wage this battle. We need further to *recognise our own weakness in it*, and the sufficient strength of Christ. Paul exhorts the Ephesians 'be strong in the Lord and in his mighty power', and gives the reason that 'our struggle is not against flesh and blood'. Were it so our own native energy might see us through. But we cannot fight the battles of the Spirit in the armour of the flesh. We need to be strong with Christ's strength.

A number of years ago, at a student conference in Holland, my host took me aside before a meeting at which I was to speak. He was a joyful Christian, one who radiated Christ's presence and peace. His friends knew him (in Dutch, naturally!) as 'Happy Harry'. He said to me, 'I hope you are going to speak to us about the life *out of Jesus Christ.*' To my ears his words sounded strange, for this was a conference of Christian students and not intended primarily for those 'out of Jesus Christ'. It was a moment before I realised that it was not my preparation nor my friend's theology which was lacking — but his use of English prepositions! He should have said, 'the life *in* Jesus Christ'. At least, that is the way the New Testament frequently describes it. Paul's most common designation of the Christian is one who is 'in Christ'. But it did not take much reflection to realise that this Dutchman had also discovered a biblical insight, for the life 'in Christ' is the life we live 'out of' Christ's supply of grace and power. It is out of the life of the vine that the strength of the branches to bear fruit flows. If that is to be realised in our lives, and specially in this matter of spiritual conflict, we must pay close attention to our Lord's words: Apart from me you can do nothing; you must therefore abide in me, press in to share in my strength and sufficiency (John 15:5).

In fact there is good reason to think that in expounding the armour of God in this passage, Paul is explaining further what he means by being strong *in the Lord*. No doubt Paul was thinking about the Roman soldier as he listed the items of the armour of God. But he was also thinking about a passage in the Old Testament which describes God himself putting on his armour and going to do battle against his enemies. When no one else would intervene, Isaiah tells us:

> so his own arm worked salvation for him, and his
> own righteousness sustained him. He put on
> righteousness as his breastplate, and the helmet of
> salvation on his head; he put on the garments of
> vengeance and wrapped himself in zeal as in a
> cloak.
>
> (Is. 59:16, 17)

It may be that with these verses as a background, Paul intends to remind us that Christ also marched into battle against the evil one. John says that the specific purpose of his coming was to 'destroy the devil's work' (1 John 3:8). What is therefore offered to the Christian, conscious of his own inadequacy for the battle, is nothing less than the armour which Christ himself wore in his battles with the enemy. It would be a valuable aid to victory in our own lives to take the time to study and meditate on the different ways in which Jesus used the armour which his Father supplied for him.

(c) In the third place, Paul tells us *why we need the armour*. Again and again (vv.11, 13, 14) he says it is in order to help us to stand. We may be inclined to think that it will enable us to reach exalted heights of Christian living, but Paul's perspective is altogether more sensible and biblical. If that is our view of the Christian life we have a very great deal yet to learn. We need everything God provides simply to remain standing. We may think it more spiritual to believe that God promises us a constant experience of Concorde-style Christian living, but if so we are taking flights into our own fantasy world and not looking into the mirror of God's word. Those who are really earnest in their concern to press on to maturity soon discover that there are days in life when it is all they can do to keep on their feet, to hold their heads above water while their hearts are crying out 'all your waves and breakers have swept over me' (Ps. 42:7).

Paul uses two expressions which reinforce this. It takes all the resources of God to keep standing because of the 'wiles of the devil' (v.11), 'the devil's schemes' as NIV translates it. One writer once tried to list these wiles in categories and illustrate them from the Bible. He ended up with 27 categories! Then there is what the apostle calls 'the day of evil' (v.13); the period to which we earlier made reference in discussing what it means to be 'led into temptation', when desire, opportunity, and temptation coincide in one dark moment, and we are conscious of being almost irresistibly drawn into sin and denial of our loyalty to Jesus Christ.

We cannot afford to underestimate the power, the demonic cleverness of Satan. We know from Scripture and experience — our own or others — that he over-reaches himself at the end of the day. But the end of the day may be a long way off from the height of the battle, and we cannot assume for a moment that we will easily escape his onslaughts. So Paul emphasises the powers which are ranged against us. They are *not* flesh and blood; rather they are *spiritual* — invisible, super-human beings, indeed immortally evil. They are also, apparently, *organised*, so that he can speak of principalities, powers, rulers, and strategies.

All this is vividly portrayed in the story of the Gadarene demoniac whose neighbours foolishly believed could be controlled by the flesh-and-blood means of ropes and chains and isolation from society. But in the face of the potential influence of Christ in that area, Satan was able to deploy a legion of demons to spearhead his attack on the kingdom of God; six thousand evil spirits sent as a fighting force from hell against the Son of God. When we realise that *this* is what we are contending against, we learn something of the marvel of having a Saviour who has bound the strong man who is armed with such weapons of terror and spiritual destruction (Mark 3:27).

We do not take this matter nearly seriously enough. But it is a key to the whole of the Christian life. Only when we recognise the forces ranged against us and see our own considerable weakness will the armour which God supplies have any real meaning in our lives. It is to this that Paul turns in the second place:

THE ARMOUR WITH WHICH WE ARE EQUIPPED

> Stand firm then, with the belt of truth buckled around your waist, with the breastplate of righteousness in place, and with your feet fitted with the readiness that comes from the gospel of

ADD TO YOUR FAITH

> peace. In addition to all this, take up the shield of
> faith, with which you can extinguish all the
> flaming arrows of the evil one. Take the helmet of
> salvation and the sword of the Spirit, which is the
> word of God. And pray in the Spirit on all
> occasions with all kinds of prayers and requests.
> With this in mind, be alert and always keep on
> praying for all the saints.
>
> (Eph. 6:14-18)

In fact we can divide 'the armour' described here into two
parts: the *preparatory* and the *military*.

(a) **Preparatory**

We are to wear the belt of truth. The belt was not, strictly
speaking, part of the soldier's armour at all. It was tied round
his under-garment in order to keep it from hindering his
movements when the armour had been donned. Otherwise he
would make no progress whatsoever. Some commentators
have suggested that Paul is thinking of the belt from which the
soldier's sword was hung. But this is unlikely, not least
because it destroys the orderliness of Paul's description. It is
better to accept the interpretation adopted by Francis Foulkes
in his commentary in the Tyndale series:

> Strictly the girdle is not part of the armour, but
> before the armour can be put on, the garments
> underneath must be bound together. The metaphor
> of girding is so often used in the Bible because it
> describes a preparatory action necessary for a
> person with the flowing garments of those days
> before work could be done, a race run, or a battle
> fought (e.g. see Luke 12:35; 1 Pet. 1:13). Isaiah 59:17
> and the description of the Christian's armour in
> 1 Thessalonians 5:8 do not mention the girdle, but
> Isaiah 11:5 says of the 'rod out of the stem of Jesse'
> that 'righteousness shall be the girdle of his loins,
> and faithfulness the girdle of his reins'
>
> *Commentary on Ephesians* p.174

But what does this belt represent in the life of the Christian?
Opinion is divided. Some writers take it to represent the truth
of God. After all, the armour is what *God* provides. But this
may be to miss the point. The truth of God is later mentioned

when Paul speaks about the 'sword of the Spirit, which is the word of God' (v.17), and, moreover, we have already seen that this belt is not really part of the armour at all. It is something which is *a prerequisite to the successful employment of the armour*. In fact the word Paul uses for truth is *alētheia* which can mean either truth or reality and faithfulness. When the Greek version of the Old Testament translated the words of David in Psalm 51:6, 'Surely you desire truth in the inner parts', it used this word *alētheia* to convey the idea of the inner integrity and sincerity before God which David had lacked when he fell into sin in one of the 'evil days' of his life. In all likelihood this is the kind of thing Paul means — reality, straightforwardness. Later in his life he was to commend Timothy for it when he spoke of his 'sincere' or 'unfeigned' faith (2 Tim. 1:5). The word he used means 'not hypocritical', 'not as a play-actor', and conveys the picture of the ancient actor, disguising the reality of his own life behind the mask actors wore in ancient times on which was portrayed the character he assumed. To emulate this in the Christian life is the high road to total disaster.

When we have said this much we have not yet exhausted what Paul means by 'truth'. For to buckle on the belt of truth, in the biblical sense, means *a willingness to apply the whole of God's word to the whole of our lives*. Without this concern to be faithful to God at every level of life we are bound to find ourselves tripped up by the enemy. Again we need go no further than the immediate context of Ephesians to find this illustrated. Witness the man who is deeply concerned about preaching and critical of anything which falls below the standard he finds in Scripture, but whose love for his wife leaves much to be desired — an angel in public, and a devil in private, as C.H. Spurgeon once put it. Or there is the wife who is interested in discussing Christian things and enjoys demonstrating her strongly held views in theology, or of the ways of God, but does not openly and clearly respect her husband and willingly show her submission to Christ by her service of him. Or there is the child who longs to win his parents for Christ but does not equally long that God will make him or her obedient and daily honouring to them in the home. Or the executive, or worker, whose Christian standards are not brought within the province of his daily labour. All this is to bring a spirit of unreality, indeed of unfaithfulness into our lives, and makes us easy prey for Satan. In fact in itself it so destroys our witness that he need do little more. The armour of God is no protection against the wiles of the devil if there is an inner, deep-seated unreality about us. What is the point of armour if the enemy has already found his way behind it and pressed his poisoned dagger into our heart?

Success in Christian warfare depends on the right preparations being made. Let us put on the belt of inner reality.

(b) **Military**

The armour of God is designed and custom-built to protect the Christian against Satan. Each piece has been forged by God with his wiles in mind. The five pieces of it which Paul mentions correspond in a significant way with five of the titles which the Bible gives to our spiritual enemy.

(i) *The Breastplate of righteousness* protects against *the Accuser*. Despite the interpretation of a number of commentators and writers, we ought to recognise that this refers primarily to our righteousness in Christ, received at conversion when we are justified by faith. The breastplate is in many ways the centre piece of the armour and guards the heart. The righteousness of Christ, given to be ours through faith, is the core of the Christian's protection from the devil. Why should this be the case? Because *the devil trades in guilt*, and the only possible defence against guilt is the defence of righteousness.

There is a very vivid illustration of this tucked away in the Old Testament book of Zechariah. In the third chapter the prophet recounts a remarkable vision he saw in which Joshua the high priest of Israel was seen standing before the angel of the Lord. Beside him stood the devil, 'at his right hand to accuse him' (Zech. 3:1). Nothing could more eloquently describe the devil's work against God's children. He is one of the great diary-keepers; he watches God's children and notes their sins and failures and then, when we are standing in the presence of God, longing to have fellowship with him as his children, he rakes up our past and brings it forward as evidence against us.

'You are no child of God', we hear him saying, 'when this, and this, and this have been true of you.' And as our past sins are brought before us we see that what he says seems to have some truth in it — yes, to be the truth. It is not for nothing that he is called 'the accuser of our brothers, who accuses them before our God day and night' (Rev. 12:10).

When we go through that kind of inner turmoil, God alone has the answer; again it is illustrated by Zechariah:

> The Lord said to Satan, "The Lord rebuke you, Satan! The Lord, who has chosen Jerusalem, rebuke you! Is not this man a burning stick snatched from the fire?'
>
> (Zech. 3:2)

This is our refuge under pressure. Let God rebuke these accusations; God has chosen us in his love, and plucked us out of our guilt and sin and condemnation. But then Zechariah adds these beautiful words:

> Now Joshua was dressed in filthy clothes as he stood before the angel. The angel said to those who were standing before him, 'Take off his filthy clothes.'
> Then he said to Joshua, 'See, I have taken away your sin, and I will put rich garments on you.' Then I said, 'Put a clean turban on his head.' So they put a clean turban on his head and clothed him, while the angel of the Lord stood by.
>
> (Zech. 3:3-5)

Meanwhile the devil had slunk away to his own place. The new garments of salvation, the gift of the clothing of the righteousness of Jesus Christ is our certain protection against this attack of Satan. That is why Martin Luther called justification, being made righteous through faith in Christ, 'the standing or falling article of the church'. When we have grasped it we have in our armoury a guard which keeps us secure. Through Christ's death and resurrection for us, all that he has done becomes ours and all our sinfulness became his. We are given through faith a perfect, complete and everlasting righteousness. We can never be any more righteous, any more justified than we are from the moment we believe. And so we are able to turn to the devil as he reads out to us the diary of our past sin, 'I do not deny it; I will not argue about it. But this I will do: I will trust, as I have trusted, in Jesus Christ, and not in my own goodness. I am not relying on what I have done for my salvation but on what he has done. Therefore, let your accusations fly, for they cannot and will not penetrate to my heart. I have put on the breastplate of righteousness.'

(ii) *Feet fitted with the readiness of the gospel of peace* protect us against *the Serpent*. Again there is some ambiguity about these words. The word translated 'readiness' in the NIV and 'preparation' in the AV can also mean 'foundation'. Paul either means that we are ready to take out the gospel of peace or that we find the gospel of peace provides us with a sure footing. It may be that both of these ideas were present in his mind, but if so it is impossible to express that in English. The more basic sense is obviously that of having a sure footing. That is necessary if we are to stand, and it is equally necessary if we are to march on with the message of salvation.

If we think of the picture of the soldier, Paul seems to be alluding to the heavy boots which gave him a sure grip, strengthened his ankles, and protected him from dangers on the ground. Is it too fanciful to think that Paul had in mind the earliest promise of the establishing of the kingdom of God and the conflict which would be created between Christ's people and the kingdom of darkness? It had been promised that the Messiah would crush the serpent's head, while it would strike at his heel (Gen. 3:15). In Romans 16:20 Paul had indicated that the conflict inaugurated between the Captain of Salvation and his Foe was continuing in the church: 'The God of peace will soon crush Satan under your feet', he had said. The boots of the peace of God would, with the help of the God of peace, crush their attacker.

It is significant that he speaks about the gospel *of peace*. It is the primary blessing of the gospel; it is therefore a prime target of the devil. He disrupts our sense that through the Cross those who believe in Christ are at peace with him — it is an established relationship, and not a matter of our emotional temperature. He tries to delude us into thinking that being at peace with God is the same as *feeling* at peace with him. *But to wear 'gospel boots' is to understand that this peace is a fact before it is a feeling*; it is a reality on which we build our experience. When the serpent whispers: 'Has God said something about peace? Surely not, for look at how upset your heart is; look at how out-of-sorts you feel', we are not obliged to enter into dialogue with him. Instead let us fix our minds on the God of peace who offers to us in Christ the peace of God. Holding to that we will use 'gospel boots' to bruise the serpent's head and maintain the enjoyment of our peace with God.

(iii) *The shield of faith* protects us against *Satan*. The shield to which Paul refers here is not the small shield for hand-to-hand combat. It is the large shield, door-like in shape and in size, which in conjunction with other shields of its kind formed a virtually impenetrable wall against the enemy. It was some four feet by two-and-a-half feet in size. It was covered with leather, because, as Paul suggests here, one of the ways the enemy might attack was by firing arrows with heads dipped in pitch and then set on fire which, when they struck their target, produced an immediate conflagration. Something large enough to give over-all protection *and* able to quench the fire was obviously necessary.

In the spiritual realm Paul suggests this shield is faith. But from what does this safeguard us? What are 'the flaming arrows of the evil one' which threaten to produce conflagration in the hearts of Christians? Part of the answer to that question is to be found in the devil's name Satan. It is as the accuser he stirs up our sense of guilt, as the serpent he disrupts our peace with God, and now as Satan that he fires these darts against us. For 'Satan' according to some scholars, comes from a root in the Aramaic language which means 'one who lies in ambush'. In other words we are to think of these arrows which set our hearts and minds and lives on fire, as coming from a hidden source. When they strike, faith is our only protection — trusting ourselves to the mercy of God and the grace of Jesus Christ.

Perhaps you are already familiar with what this means. If you are the knowledge that this is how Satan works is half the battle. From time to time, some Christians have found thoughts and feelings in their lives like raging fires gone out of control.

They are often enough sinful, distasteful thoughts and temptations. We do not know where they have come from and so we naturally assume they have emerged from our own hearts. We know that out of the heart proceeds all manner of evil and so that is the inevitable conclusion we draw. Is this not what Scripture itself teaches? But that is only a partial truth, and partial truth can verge on falsehood; for Satan also knows and uses Scripture for his own fiendish ends. *He* has planted these thoughts in our minds — the fact that we hate them is evidence that they are not ours. Now, from his hidden position it seems he is able to lead us to thinking this is our own sin.

C. H. Spurgeon the nineteenth century Baptist preacher tells how as a young man he had to put his hand to his mouth to prevent himself physically from uttering hideous language. Yet, he says, he had never heard an oath in his life. This is Satan's work.

A friend once confessed to me that for a period of many weeks he found his mind filled with blasphemous thoughts. He believed that he had been called to minister God's word; his friends were convinced of his vocation and he was preparing himself for that work. But how could God call a man with thoughts like his? He was almost broken in pieces by this hidden secret which he felt he could share with nobody. Had he backslidden? Or actually committed the unforgivable sin? Was he, studying for the work of the ministry of the gospel, actually an apostate? Had he crucified the Son of God afresh on his own account? But the true interpretation of his experience was for a long time hidden from him. He was being spiritually ambushed; Satan was sowing these thoughts in his mind, producing a fire which could scarcely be put out. In the midst of this fiery furnace all he could do was hold on in faith to Christ, believing that he could and would forgive someone like him.

That kind of experience, especially in the lives of those who are called to some similar ministry, is probably far more common than is generally imagined. Readers of *The Pilgrim's Progress* have often found that John Bunyan shared it, in what we may assume is a deeply autobiographical passage:

> One thing I could not let slip: I took notice that now
> poor *Christian* was so confounded, that he did not
> know his own voice: And thus I perceived it: Just
> when he was come over against the mouth of the
> burning Pit, one of the Wicked Ones got behind
> him, and stepped up softly to him, and
> whisperingly suggested grievous blasphemies to
> him, which he verily thought had proceeded from
> his own mind. This put *Christian* more to it than
> anything that he met with before, even to think
> that he should now blaspheme him that he loved so
> much before; yet if he could have helped it, he
> would not have done it: But he had not the
> discretion either to stop his ears, or to know from
> whence those blasphemies came.

For such an onslaught we need a large shield to quench the
fiery darts of the devil. Such a shield is faith in Christ:

> When all around my soul gives way,
> He then is all my hope and stay.
> On Christ, the solid rock I stand;
> All other ground is sinking sand.

(iv) *The helmet of salvation* protects us against *the Deceiver*.
The Roman soldier's helmet gave him protection for the head,
but it also provided him with dignity and identity. He was a
representative of Rome, a soldier in his General's army.
Nobody could face him and his comrades without recognising
that they faced the might of a great Empire, embodied and
represented in this single figure of the Roman soldier. In a
similar sense, we can understand Paul here to be thinking of
'salvation' in its fullest biblical sense. The believer's immediate
salvation in conflict with his enemy is the assurance of the
dignity and new identity that God has given to him in Christ.

In particular, this is our defence against the evil one as the
Deceiver. Scripture speaks of the deceitfulness of sin, and
behind that deception lies the figure of the arch-deceiver. He
leads the whole world astray, says John in Revelation 12:9. He
may even appear as an angel of light, says Paul, but we are not
to be taken in by him (2 Cor. 11:14).

This deception may take place in two ways. The *first*, and in
some ways the worst, is by blackmail. It is a characteristic

subtlety of the devil that he uses this means — in which the
price of keeping our sin secret is an increasing yielding to his
ways. How many Christians, rather than allow one fatal error
to come out into the open — to be shared perhaps with other
Christians and forgiven, so that not only reconciliation can
take place, but acceptance, strength and spiritual
rehabilitation may be received — have listened to the evil one's
guarantees that all may be covered over . . . but only at the price
of continuing in bondage to him. For such temptations we need
a clear mind; a mind protected by the helmet of God's
salvation, and by an understanding that salvation is precisely
this — being saved from sin and guilt and past shame. How
often the devil gets Christians in a corner because they are
forced back into a position of believing that God and their
fellow-believers accept them on the grounds of their own
righteousness. We must throw that lie back in the face of the
Blackmailer and firmly fix the helmet of salvation in place.

The second way in which this deception takes place is by a
more direct attack on our identity, involving less disobedience
and more forgetfulness. We lose sight of the privileges which
are ours as heirs of God's grace, or we find that Satan mounts a
frontal attack to deny them. This has been his plan from the
beginning. In the Garden of Eden he sowed doubts in the mind
of Adam and Eve that they really were the loved and cared for
children that God said they were. 'If that were so', insinuated
Satan, 'God would never have kept back from you what he has
done.' In the wilderness of Judea his accents were heard by the
Last Adam — 'If you are the Son of God . . . If you are the Son of
God . . .', still seeking to plant doubts about his Father's love
and the reality of his own unique relationship to him. On his
head Christ placed the helmet of salvation. In his case he was
the maker of it. In our case we are the recipients of it. With such
a dignity and identity we are assured of standing in the evil
day.

(v) *The Sword of the Spirit* protects us against *the Lier*. The
truth of God, the word of God, says Paul, is both our defence
and our weapon of warfare. We need to know it and to employ
it because it enables us to battle against *the Lier*. Satan has no
qualms about twisting the truth, diverting its sharp edge, even

openly contradicting it when it fits his purposes to do so. But a knowledge of God's word exposes his true nature, and enables us to discern his hand where by human gaze it cannot be seen. This is the truly remarkable thing about the way in which the Spirit enables us to use the sword he has given us. We see his gracious influence in his working on us by the word for our growth in grace — he makes us sensitive to the lies of the devil. There may be times when we are scarcely able to put into words the suspicions we have in some situations. But as we trust in the teaching of Scripture, as we sit under the ministry of it, we find that the entrance of God's word gives us light; it imparts understanding to the simple (Ps.119:130), and through its illuminating power we recognise the strategies of evil, and are enabled to defeat them.

Being a Christian means being a soldier. We have been brought into heavenly realms in Christ. But that is where the action is, and it is important, if we are to grow strong and stand, that we should realise that the two great principles of military warfare are also the two great principles of Christian warfare:

1. KNOW YOUR ENEMY   2. KNOW YOUR RESOURCES

When we grasp these two principles of living the Christian life, it will become clear to us why Isaiah spoke of the influence of God's strength producing an unexpected pattern in the life of the believer:

> He gives strength to the weary
> and increases the power of
> the weak.
> Even youths grow tired and
> weary,
> and young men stumble and
> fall;
> but those who hope in the
> Lord
> will renew their strength.
> They will soar on wings like
> eagles;
> they will run and not grow
> weary,
> they will walk and not be
> faint.
>
> (Is. 40:29-31)

In the light of what Paul says about Christian warfare as part of our progress to maturity, we might well add:

And in the evil day,
They will stand.

9

Coping with suffering

When we examine the New Testament's teaching on Christian maturity we discover that it places considerable emphasis on the necessity for *steady* growth.

But we should not imagine that *growth* is something which develops at an even pace. Many of the pictures we find in Scripture to illustrate it are horticultural and biological. They do not suggest the invariable progress of the mechanical. Plants develop through a variety of influences which are not constant. Children certainly do — and it is not uncommon for friends of a family to comment on how a boy or girl seems to have 'shot up' in a short space of time, when in previous months their development had been imperceptibly steady.

It is important then for us to recognise that in our Christian development there will be critical periods, perhaps one experience which will bring our lives to such a point of crisis that much of our future growth will depend on our response to it. One such crisis is that of suffering, of tribulation or affliction. No study of Christian maturity would be complete without recognising that for many Christians this is a matter of major importance. It is recognised as such in the New Testament. Paul tells the Philippians that they not only have the privilege of believing in Christ but of suffering for him (Phil. 1:29). He emphasises that it is only through *tribulation* that we will enter the kingdom of God. The word 'tribulation' is a very interesting one. The *tribulum* was the Roman threshing implement, separating the wheat from the chaff. It presents a picture of the pains which may be involved in growing in grace. The word Paul actually uses is *thlipsis* which means heavy pressure. Anything which presses us down to the limit is 'tribulation'. It will be readily agreed that it plays a major role in spiritual life. With Moses we must choose suffering with Christ rather than the pleasures of Egypt (Heb. 11:25); with Paul we must see the importance of longing that we might share in the fellowship of Christ's sufferings too (Phil. 3:10).

How then are we to react to suffering if we are to press on in the Christian race? Most of us tend to react to it in one of two ways. On the one hand, after we have come through the darkness we may well find that within a comparatively short space of time our experience is a thing of the past. We say 'thank goodness that's over', and soon the deep impressions we felt it had made upon us seem to be little more than faded memories. It plays little significance in our future. On the other hand, it is possible to find ourselves strangely bound to such an experience so that we cannot let it go — nor does it let us go. We can never forget it; we do not want to forget it; and we develop a fixation about it. Some loss or disappointment or suffering in our lives then becomes the focal point of our whole personalities and we live in its light for years to come. We feed our minds and emotions on it until they become poisoned with a spirit of bitterness and our whole personalities become warped because we have not been able to cope with the crisis of suffering.

In this chapter attention is focused on two parts of Scripture which are particularly helpful in this area. The first is part of the psalm described earlier as 'The Psalm of Maturity', Psalm 119; the second is the well-known passage in Paul's Second Letter to the Corinthians in which he transcribes his personal testimony to God's help in a time of great suffering.

THE PSALM OF MATURITY REVISITED — PSALM 119

> Before I was afflicted I went astray,
> but now I obey your word. (v.67)

> It was good for me to be afflicted
> so that I might learn your decrees. (v.71)

I know, O Lord, that your laws are righteous
and in faithfulness you have afflicted me. (v.75)

To be able to say 'It was good for me me to be afflicted' is a mark of maturity. This older believer, passing on some of the lessons he had learned in his long life of faith in God, avoided the two errors of forgetfulness and fixation. He looked beyond his experience of suffering to see the hand of God, and wherever his hand could be discerned permitting and providing the circumstances of his life, he was persuaded nothing but good could result from a willing acceptance of his afflictions. Of course he was not speaking for all. Not all are able to say what he said; not all benefit from affliction. But he did, and so should every child of God.

The reason the psalmist was able to express his feelings in this wonderful way is explained later in the same psalm. He tells us that he would have perished in his afflictions 'If your law had not been my delight' (v.92). That was particularly true under the added pressures of unbelieving men around him — 'Where's your God of love now?' they would say, smearing him with lies (v.69). But he himself had learned what he wants to pass on to others — that there is wisdom, guidance and interpretation of life in the word of God which will see us through even the darkest of our experiences. Such blessings may be hardly won. But they are assured to those who wait on God and trust in his promises. The particular benefits and blessings he mentions in verses 67, 71, and 75 are three-fold.

(a) **His sufferings revealed his spiritual needs (v.67).** In our daily contact with others we sometimes discover that only a crisis brings out their true character. Some of our friends who sail through life with a mild and placid disposition can show a quite different face when contradicted or insulted. Then appears from some secret part of their souls a venomous temper. Some of our most timid acquaintances can show a nerve of steel in unexpected ways. In a rather similar way for the Christian, his suffering can unravel for him as well as others, the stuff of which he is made. Here was a man, in Psalm 119, who was enjoying considerable material prosperity. Life was full and satisfying. But he did not see that his natural prosperity was disguising his spiritual bankruptcy. Not that there is anything wrong with prosperity. It is an excellent servant. But it so easily becomes a totalitarian master. And only in a moment of need does it stand revealed as a master unable to provide for us. So this man's affliction awakened him to his inner spiritual poverty. Before he was afflicted *he went astray*. He was not openly rebelling against God — presumably his close friends saw the same outwardly devoted servant of God. But inwardly his heart was no longer set on the enthronement of God in his life. He had been captured by an alien idol — prosperity.

How easily this happens! Jesus paints the picture of it in his parable of the Sower and the soils. Some seed fell among thorns; as yet unnoticed, but nonetheless present, and potentially destructive of good seed. So it is that the cares of this world and the delight or pleasure in riches devour the fruit of the gospel and it never reaches maturity and fruitfulness. Failure to do the weeding is the only prerequisite. Psalm 119 tells us of a man who was brought to his senses by a sharp pain to realise that there was much weeding to be done in his heart if God was to be honoured there. Many Christians testify to the same experience: 'We would not know where we would have been spiritually had we not been brought low by this suffering.'

Of course it needs to be emphasised that not all suffering is intended as a warning against spiritual decline. We are called to suffer for righteousness' sake by Christ (Matt. 5:11). We share in the sufferings of others because we are one with them in Christ (1 Cor. 12:26). But there are times in our experience when this is the case; when we are drifting towards the rocks and in danger of making shipwreck of our faith. The mercy is that God does not leave us to drift. He sends out his lifeboat, of which the coxswain may be the dark figure of affliction. But he alone can carry us back to port and we therefore need to learn George Matheson's secret:

> O joy that seekest me through pain
> I dare not ask to fly from thee.

(b) **His sufferings taught him the ways of God (v.71).** It is not everyone who can say 'It was good for me to be afflicted'. This does not mean the Christian enjoys suffering in some perverse, masochistic way. On the contrary, 'No discipline seems pleasant at the time, but painful' (Heb. 12:11). What it means is that affliction may do us good, in this particular sense that it teaches us 'the decrees of God'. It is unlikely that this means what theologians often call 'God's eternal decree' when they are discussing predestination and election. Rather it means the great principles which God has decreed belong to the spiritual life. This is primarily what is meant by the 'goodness' which the psalmist discovered in his affliction. He came to experience in his own life the power of truths he had long known, and now learned experimentally what he had for so long known only intellectually. Martin Luther put it like this: 'I never knew the meaning of God's word until I came into affliction. I have always found it one of my best schoolmasters.' 'Affliction', he says elsewhere, 'is the Christian's theologian' — it teaches him what nothing else can.

But how does this come about? For one thing it focuses our attention on the things that really matter, enables us to weigh our own lives in the divine balances and make the adjustments which are often clearly necessary. For another, it confirms for us God's determination to draw us as close as possible to himself, to make us more conscious of our dependence on him — whatever the cost. C. S. Lewis captures this lesson in his exquisite way, when he says:

> Imagine yourself as a living house. God comes in to rebuild that house. At first, perhaps, you understand what he is doing. He is getting the drains right, and stopping the leaks in the roof, and so on: you knew that those jobs needed doing, and so you are not surprised.
>
> But presently he starts knocking the house about in a way that hurts abominably and does not seem to make sense. What on earth is he up to? The explanation is that he is building a quite different house from the one you thought of — throwing up a wing there, putting up an extra floor there, running up towers, making courtyards. You thought you were going to be made into a decent little cottage; but he is building a palace. He intends to come and live in it himself.
>
> *Mere Christianity* p.172

God is willing to go to any lengths with us to make us like his Son. That is ultimately the goal of our maturity. And it is often only in the fires of affliction, when we sense the strong hand of God holding us up, that we come to appreciate his ways with us and the gracious decree that lies behind the principle that only through tribulation do we enter the kingdom of God.

(c) **His sufferings showed him the faithfulness of God (v.75).** God had afflicted him in faithfulness. At first glance we might think the writer means that he was simply getting his just deserts. After all, he himself admitted that he was going astray. Is he now simply confessing that the suffering he has gone through has been 'the punishment to fit the crime'? If that had been so he would have written instead, '*In justice* you have afflicted me.' But it is not God's justice in the experience which is central for him; it is the faithfulness of God which has so clearly been revealed to him through the darkness of affliction. No doubt before it all he would have feared suffering as a potential destroyer of his faith and trust in God, and a threat to God's very purpose of blessing in his life. But now, through it all, he had come to recognise that in his great faithfulness God employs these trials as instruments of his blessing, in order to fulfil his will through them. They are not threats to God's purpose, but further indications of how meticulously faithful he is to that purpose.

The life of Joseph provides one clear illustration of this. As a young man he had been marked out by God for leadership among his people. God intimated to him in a dream that he would do an unusual work through him. But in his pride he made God's grace the servant of his own self-interest and preoccupation. In his heart he went astray, and then followed apparent disaster followed by suffering, followed by apparent disaster. But at the end of the day he was exalted to a position of supreme influence in Egypt and the dream that his family would one day bow before him to acknowledge his power was fulfilled. But what is more important is the lesson Joseph learned. It is eloquently expressed in his words to his brothers about his tribulations: 'You intended to harm me, but God intended it for good to accomplish what is now being done ...' (Gen. 50:20). He would have been able to say with the author of

Psalm 119: 'Thou hast dealt well with thy servant, O Lord, according to thy word' (v.65, RSV).

The Psalm of Maturity sets out for us basic principles. It does not at any point specify the precise nature of the suffering, and what it says can therefore be applied to all suffering. In fact the word translated 'affliction' is a very general term which can refer to anything which brings us low, humbles us and makes us feel small and inadequate. To this general teaching we can add the very specific illustration of suffering about which the apostle Paul speaks in 2 Corinthians 12:7-10.

PAUL — THE CHRONIC SUFFERER

We are apt to think of Paul in a number of fairly stereo-typed ways. He was 'the converted persecutor' — and that aspect of his life was certainly a dominant one in his own self-understanding; he was also 'the mighty evangelist', conscious that this was the great task of his life, to preach the gospel where it had never before been heard, and to discharge the debt he owed to men as the recipient of good news and salvation. Again, Paul can be seen as 'the master theologian', hammering out in his letters the revelation given to him by Christ and applying it to every situation arising in the early church, in the consciousness of his special role as an apostle of Christ to pass on the 'pattern of sound words' which would build the church and evangelise the world. All of these pictures of Paul, especially when taken together, are accurate.

But we rarely present the picture of Paul which we are given in 2 Corinthians 12. That is not surprising really, because Paul himself rarely speaks of this aspect of his life as *Paul — the chronic sufferer*. Yet at the very beginning of his ministry this was the prophetic word pronounced over his life by his Lord: 'I will show him how much he must suffer for my name' (Acts 9:16). Little did he realise then how many different ways those words would find their fulfilment. When, years later, he wrestled with the pride and failure of the church at Corinth he was constrained to open his heart to them, he described one very special affliction in these words:

J

I know a man in Christ who fourteen years ago was caught up to the third heaven. Whether it was in the body or out of the body I do not know — God knows. And I know that this man — whether in the body or apart from the body I do not know, but God knows — was caught up to Paradise. He heard inexpressible things, things that man is not permitted to tell. I will boast about a man like that, but I will not boast about myself, except about my weaknesses. Even if I should choose to boast, I would not be a fool, because I would be speaking the truth. But I refrain, so no-one will think more of me than is warranted by what I do or say.

To keep me from becoming conceited because of these surpassingly great revelations, there was given me a thorn in my flesh, a messenger of Satan to torment me. Three times I pleaded with the Lord to take it away from me. But he said to me, "My grace is sufficient for you, for my power is made perfect in weakness." Therefore I will boast all the more gladly about my weaknesses, so that Christ's power may rest on me. That is why, for Christ's sake, I delight in weaknesses, in insults, in hardships, in persecutions, in difficulties. For when I am weak, then I am strong.

(2 Cor. 12:2-10)

There are several important features in Paul's experience which are worth noting.

(a) **The reality of his suffering.** The strength of the expressions he employs should rid our minds of any vestige of doubt about whether the Christian can suffer. He tells us that his affliction was a 'thorn'. The word can also mean a sharp stake. Inevitably there has been a long-standing debate about the precise nature of this 'thorn', and the suggestions made have been almost as numerous as the scholars who have made them — and sometimes the very ailments from which these writers have suffered themselves! Possibly the oldest tradition is that, whatever the precise nature of the illness, the 'thorn' to which Paul refers was the piercing headache which accompanied it. A famous scholar of earlier this century, Sir William Ramsey, suggested in his book *St Paul the Traveller and the Roman Citizen* that the apostle may have suffered from a species of chronic malaria fever which issued in distressing and prostrating paroxysms which would strike him particularly when special effort was required. Certainly that would fit in with some of the things he writes in his letters to the Corinthians and the Galatians. 'Within my experience', wrote Ramsey, 'several persons innocent of Pauline theorising, have described it as: like a red hot bar thrust through the forehead.'

The point is, whatever the nature of the illness, it was not simply an inconvenience, or an irritation. *It was an agony.* He says it was given 'to torment me' — the expression comes from the Greek for a clenched fist. He was 'cuffed' by it, beaten black and blue. If not yet destroyed, he was certainly struck down (2 Cor. 4:9).

The thorn was *painful* because it was *physical.* It was *in his flesh.* Here he is not using the Greek word *sarx* (as he does elsewhere) to signify man in his sinful condition and corruption. He is speaking about his body, his flesh and blood. This pain he felt was not only mental, but experienced in the body. It made him feel his physical weaknesses. Perhaps it is this he refers to again in the earlier letter to the Galatians: 'As you know it was because of an illness that I first preached the gospel to you. Even though my illness was a trial to you, you did not treat me with contempt or scorn [the fear of the man whose weakness is obviously physical] . . . I can testify that, if you could have done so, you would have torn out your eyes and given them to me [a possible reference to the effect his illness had on his vision?]' (Gal. 4:13, 15). It is not impossible that this physical suffering added personal poignancy to what Paul had written in 2 Corinthians 5:1, 2 about the new body which believers would receive in glory — 'Meanwhile we groan . . .'; and what he had just said in 2 Corinthians 10:10 — 'in person he [Paul] is unimpressive'. Any reader who has known a crippling physical disability finds a brother sufferer in this man.

What then did Paul do? He did the most natural thing in the world. He cried out for deliverance: 'I pleaded with the Lord to take it away from me.' 'Jesus, Lord, help me!' The great apostle became like Bartimaeus, crying out for mercy and relief. Three times he cried. Three times what he specifically requested, 'Take it away', was refused. It is extremely likely that we are

meant to see here more than a reminder of Bartimaeus. The
One to whom Paul cried had also once prayed three times for
the cause of impending suffering to be removed: 'My Father, if
it is possible, *let this cup pass from me.*' That is meant to teach
us a great lesson and provide vital comfort to sufferers. It is not
always necessarily sinful to wrestle with the will of God and to
ask for something he will not grant us at the end of the day.
How dismal a view of God we would have if we pictured him
chiding Paul in his agony! No, *wrestling* with God's will is
often necessary for the sufferer. It is only *rebellion* that is
wrong. As we grow in grace and our spiritual faculties develop
through exercise, we learn to know ourselves with sufficient insight to distinguish one from the other, the good from the evil.
But of principal importance for our growth is the appreciation
that this kind of real suffering may come our way. The fatal
mistake is to blind ourselves to the possibility.

(b) **The instrument of his suffering.** Paul regarded his illness as
a messenger. He uses the word 'angel'. But not all angels are
good and he recognised that this one came from Satan. He
thereby teaches us an important lesson: *we should recognise
Satan's hand in much of our suffering.* That is one of the
lessons of the book of Job in the Old Testament. The anguish of
his condition was magnified for him because of the
interpretation his friends placed on his suffering. They said,
essentially: 'You are suffering because you have sinned, and
God is the author of your suffering.' But the message of the
book, as the opening chapters make clear, is that Job was
suffering not for sin but for righteousness; the instrument of
his suffering was not God, but Satan. In fact, Satan was living
up to his title — and 'ambushing' Job from a place so well-
hidden that Job and his friends mistook his activity for that of
God.
    What was Satan's purpose in all this? It was to twist the
heart of Paul from love for his Lord, just as it was to drive the
hapless Job from the comforts of God's presence. How nearly
he succeeded in Job's case:

> Surely, O God, you have worn me out;
> you have devastated my entire household.
> You have bound me — and it has become a witness;

> my gauntness rises up and testifies against me.
> God assails me and tears me in his anger
> and gnashes his teeth at me ...
> All was well with me, but he shattered me;
> he seized me by the neck and crushed me.
> He has made me his target ...
>
> (Job 16:7-9, 12)

Like another saint in the old dispensation, he felt that God had 'taken me up and thrown me aside' (Ps. 102:10).

But the truth of the matter was that it was not God who had done all this, and by his deceitful disguise, all the hatred which should have been directed towards Satan, was beginning to turn upon Job's only refuge. We cannot doubt that the same demonic strategy was at work in Paul's experience. The difference was that Paul discerned that alien presence, and resorted to prayer (not, interestingly, to exorcism).

At the same time, Paul balances that insight with another. *He recognised God's purposes in his suffering.* He tells us that this thorn 'was given' to him. The verb he uses invariably has God as its subject in the letters of Paul — as for example in 1 Cor. 11:15; 12:7, 8; Gal. 3:21; Eph. 3:7. Not even this pain could be his without divine permission. So he came to recognise that the hand inflicting the wound was Satan's, but the purpose which was being gloriously fulfilled was God's.

I have a close friend whose upbringing of his children illustrates this rather well. He never chastises them with his own hand. It is always the slipper he uses. In his view the hand of the father is for provision and direction — and so rather than use it directly for punishment or correction, he lifts up the slipper. How very important for us to see that Satan, for all his power and in all the pain he is able to inflict is but the slipper of God. Undoubtedly a slipper with a mind and will of its own! But nonetheless never able, ultimately, to escape from his unwilling end of fulfilling the sovereign purposes of God.

In Paul's case the fact that he saw *Satan's hand* guarded him from bitterness against God. The fact that he saw *God's purpose* guarded him from despair, and from fearing that this pain would end in his own destruction. It was when he began to grasp this that his experience made sense.

(c) **The reason for his suffering.** Earlier, in the principles we
saw brought out in Psalm 119, we noticed how suffering can
produce blessing. Paul gives us a rather unusual side-light on
that principle. It seems that part of the reason for his affliction
was to enable him to contain blessing. That, unhesitatingly,
may be singled out as a genuine mark of increased maturity.
Many Christians to whom God has come in a special way have
allowed the seeds of spiritual decay to grow in their souls
because they have not contained the blessing within a well
grounded biblical life-style. The blessing received has become
everything, and, as was true of the Corinthian Christians, it has
not been stabilised by a clear understanding of God's purposes.
This is not to say that such blessing, be it experimental or
intellectual, emotional or doctrinal, is insignificant. It is not —
least of all for the recipient. But babies do not grow either by
the enlargement of their heads or by the moving of their
emotions. True growth takes place in every part of us, and
lasting growth necessitates that all the members of the body
grow together. Intellectual growth needs to be contained by
increasing physical capability, and vice-versa. So in the life of
the Spirit.

Paul had known a unique blessing. He had seen what could
never be shared with any mortal. Now he had to illustrate
himself that 'we have this treasure in jars of clay to show that
this all-surpassing power is from God and not from us' (2 Cor.
4:7). He was given a thorn in the flesh 'to keep me from being
conceited'. God knew him; God knew his tendencies; God
prized Paul's continuing fruitfulness. And so he was given this
clay container, so easily broken, so unimpressive to see — in
order that God might have all the glory. We need only review
the servants of God in past and present generations to see what
a constant principle of God's ways with men this is. There are
few fruitful men and women whose lives do not hide hidden
pain. How else could their usefulness be contained and
advanced?

But Paul was not only kept humble through this thorn in his
flesh. Through it he learned in experience the sufficiency of
God's grace. Perhaps this is the most important thing of all. He
was, after all, the apostle of grace. He contended in his letters
for the full, free grace of God, unfettered by the works of man.

Yet there was grace of which he yet knew little. There is a supply of grace which we do not know until we stand in felt need of it — 'grace sufficient'. Paul could not learn it on the Damascus Road, or in Arabia. It could only be learned in the loneliness of personal affliction. In that school he had been enrolled, perhaps more than a decade before this narrative of his experience was drawn reluctantly from him. There he had learned of God's power resting on his weakness. There he had been taught how God spells 'grace'. It was the same lesson John Newton later learned and described in words so expressive of the personal experience of the famous theologian P. T. Forsyth, that he regarded them 'almost as holy writ'. Newton wrote this, in his hymn 'Prayer answered by Crosses':

> I asked the Lord that I might grow
> In faith and love and every grace
> Might more of his salvation know
> And seek more earnestly his face.
>
> 'Twas he who taught me thus to pray
> And he, I trust, has answered prayer,
> But it has been in such a way
> As almost drove me to despair.
>
> I thought that in some favoured hour
> At once he'd answer my request
> And by his love's constraining power
> Subdue my sins and give me rest.
>
> Instead of this he made me feel
> The hidden evils of my heart
> And bade the angry powers of hell
> Assault my soul in every part.
>
> Nay more, with his own hand he seemed
> Intent to aggravate my woe,
> Crossed all the fair designs I schemed
> Blasted my gourds, and laid me low.
>
> Lord, why is this? I trembling cried
> Wilt thou pursue this worm to death?
> This is the way, the Lord replied,
> I answer prayer for grace and faith.
>
> These inward trials I employ
> From self and sin to set thee free
> And cross thy schemes of earthly joy
> That thou might'st find thy all in me.

'God meant it for good!'

We find then that Paul experienced Christ's power in a new and unexpected way. He learned also that through the mystery of our own suffering there sometimes develops *a ministry to those who suffer*. All he says to the Corinthians is prefaced by his consciousness that the comfort he has received from God is his only enabling to comfort others who are in any distress (2 Cor. 1:3-7).

What then does it mean to be a mature Christian in suffering? It means to come, eventually, to see what Paul saw — that even in these experiences we can learn to be contented in Christ. He would boast of his weakness if only it meant that Christ's power would be seen. Indeed, he delighted in it, for when he was weak in himself he was strong in Christ. He discovered, like Samuel Rutherford that 'some graces grow best in winter'. And supremely he found in such trials his greatest ambition, fellowship with the Lord Jesus Christ, fulfilled. Had he not once written, 'All I care for is to know Christ . . . to share the fellowship of his sufferings, being made like him in his death'? (Phil. 3:10). Here, now, he was most like him. Christ too had the thorn. He too had prayed three times for its removal. He too had discovered the sufficiency of God's grace. He too had seen God's power flow from his weakness. The messenger of Satan sent to buffet him in the Cross became the instrument of God for man's salvation. The stake on which Christ was impaled became the triumphal chariot of his conquest.

For Paul, as for us, it is under the shadow of Calvary that we find the mystery of our suffering transformed into a ministry. We do not yet understand, but we know that Christ's greater suffering makes sense of our lesser suffering. We know too that it is in fellowship with that Great Sufferer that our own experience of suffering may lead us to a greater Christian maturity.

Pressing on

Pressing on

10
Serving faithfully

On a number of occasions in our study of the biblical teaching on Christian maturity we have noticed the recurring emphasis that links true spiritual growth with a life that is given in service to others.

Perhaps an illustration may serve to illuminate this principle. Many people enjoy watching ballet. They marvel at the agility and sustained strength of the dancers, and when in secret they become famous ballerinas themselves, they wonder how such physical contortions can be endured. One of the reasons is that ballet students are taught to employ their bodies in a quite different way from the way we normally use them. For ballet the body has to be *externally rotated*. The ballet dancer's body moves outwardly rather than inwardly. That is why after long years of ballet-dancing a ballerina's walk may be faintly reminiscent of a duck! Now, after years of life moving with a body rotation one way — what a painful trial it is to reverse its rotation! But without that basic reversal no ballet is possible. Any efforts to dance *Swan Lake* will end up with a prematurely 'dying swan'! 'The Sugar Plum Fairy' will be more like the rumble of an elephant!

In the Christian life, the beauty of true maturity, the grace of a life fully grown in Christ is only possible where that life is also 'externally rotated'; where it is directed upwards to God and outwards to our neighbour. Only when we have gone through the painful process of reversing our natural life-style, our spiritually immature self-centredness, internal rotation, can we ever hope to press on in the Christian life.

We have already mentioned two New Testament letters where internal rotation had produced spiritual forces in danger of driving the congregation to the verge of a spiritual precipice — 1 Corinthians and Hebrews.

The Corinthians

In reading through the First Letter to the Corinthians one of the saddening features which emerges is how wrongly they estimated their own spiritual condition. *They were radically confused about the marks of maturity.*

(a) *In the first place* they valued men more than their message. Paul speaks in this context about the quarrelling which resulted because of their 'jealousy' (1 Cor. 3:3). What exactly was this jealousy? The word is *zēlos*, and in other places is translated by the English word *zeal*. In fact this was what their jealousy amounted to — *a misplaced zeal for men, and the way in which God spoke through them.* There is something very sinister and frightening taking place when a Christian exhibits that kind of jealousy. I have seen it several times in connection with preachers — a devotion to them and their emphasis which makes it impossible for their admirers to profit from the preaching and teaching of anyone else. Unfortunately that is sometimes encouraged by preachers who want to monopolise the affections of their hearers. But whether this be the case or not, it is invariably detrimental, and *it is never a sign of maturity.* That requires stressing for frequently 'the ministry we enjoy' is the proud boast of such 'zealous' Christians, and it is assumed that receiving such a ministry is the equivalent of growing to maturity. To so conclude is itself a sign of how far from that maturity we really are. John Angell James, a minister in Birmingham, England during the nineteenth century and in his day a household word among Christians put his finger on the same mistake in wise and balanced words which have abiding relevance:

> a growing attachment to some particular preacher
> ... is not always of itself a proof of progress in
> religion. We are allowed our preference even in this
> matter: for though it is the message rather than the

> messenger — the truth rather than the preacher —
> that is to be the ground of our attachment, yet it
> cannot in the nature of things be otherwise than
> that we should prefer one minister to another. He
> may have been the instrument of our conversion,
> or the means of our establishment; or,
> independently of these matters, he may more
> clearly explain, and more powerfully enforce God's
> truth ... But nothing in a young convert requires
> greater care and effort *to keep down excess*, than
> ministerial attachment, *lest it should degenerate
> into exclusiveness and spiritual idolatry. They
> make this pulpit favourite not only the standard of
> all excellence but its monopolist.*
>
> *Christian Progress* p. 110

(b) *In the second place,* the Corinthians valued the personal *reception* of spiritual gifts above *the employment of those gifts for others;* they placed a premium on *abilities* rather than on *loving.* Indeed Paul says again they were zealots (1 Cor. 14:12) when it came to spiritual gifts. The innuendo is that they had given their affections to a false and self-centred set of values. Whereas the first mistake resulted in childishness instead of maturity, Paul's emphasis here is that *they were puffed up instead of being built up.* There is a very definite contrast between these two ideas in 1 Corinthians. Paul told them that they were 'God's building' (1 Cor. 3:9). He had laid the foundation, and others had built it up (1 Cor. 3:10). In this short section (1 Cor. 3:9-15), the 'building' family of words is used no less than five times. Paul at least had tried to build them up. They should have learned from his example that 'Knowledge puffs up, but love builds up' (1 Cor. 8:1). Later on in the letter he emphasises that this is the real purpose for which God gave the gifts of the Spirit to the church (1 Cor. 14:3, 4, 5, 12, 17, 26). In the light of that they are not to be children in their attitudes (1 Cor. 14:20). But instead of being built up as Christians, their size was really a bad guide to their maturity. They were 'puffed up' - their growth was produced by a lack of true nourishment and was not an indication of strength (1 Cor. 4:6, 18, 19; 5:2; 8:1; 13:4). These Christians who felt themselves to be at an advanced stage of maturity were causing their father in Christ

painful concern (1 Cor. 4:14-16), because he saw that *they were
not growing up to adult Christian living.*

But the Corinthians were not alone.

The Hebrews

Earlier in our studies, in chapter two, we saw how the writer of
Hebrews seems to change gear between the end of chapter five
and the beginning of chapter six. At the end of chapter five he is
speaking of the symptoms of spiritual immaturity, while in
chapter six he turns his attention to the danger of possible
apostasy. The danger we saw previously was that of failing to
press on so that few signs of grace are left in our lives. But it is
just here that the writer puts his finger on one of the subtle
dangers which these Hebrews may well have shared with the
Corinthians. They had an inveterate tendency to confuse true
and false marks of maturity.

In Hebrews 6:4, 5, those who have professed repentance (but
at the end of the day may not persevere in true faith) are
assumed to share in five characteristics: (1) they have been
enlightened, (2) they have tasted the heavenly gift, (3) they
have shared in the Holy Spirit, (4) they have tasted the
goodness of the word of God, and (5) they have tasted the
powers of the coming age. It may be worth asking in passing
why these early Christians put things this way, and why we
today might not think of any of these marks if asked what the
external signs of Christian faith are.

The Hebrews probably assumed that these five things were
without doubt marks of spiritual progress. But the writer of the
letter obviously held another, more biblical view, and while
scarcely two commentators can be found to agree in their
definitions of the precise significance of these phrases, in
general terms it is not difficult to relate them to common
spiritual experience.

They had been enlightened. Early in the history of the church
that phrase came to be synonymous with *baptism.* Certainly it
is a description of one aspect of the transformation which
baptism symbolises in the opening of the eyes of our
understanding (2 Cor. 4:4-6; Eph. 1:18 etc.) The message of the
gospel has a powerful influence on the minds of people brought
up in a culture with centuries of Christian tradition; how much

more so on those who waited for the Light of the World almost from the dawn of creation. Yet it is possible to meet people whose minds have been arrested *by the power of the truth*, but whose hearts have never been really broken and renewed *by the influences of grace*. A change of mind is not necessarily a mark of spiritual progress.

They had tasted the heavenly gift. Some commentators like to join this with the idea of enlightenment as baptism, and interpret these words as a reference to the Lord's Supper. The early Christians however, did not so understand them. The heavenly gift may be the Holy Spirit, or more generally, the blessings of the gospel. We may think for example of Simon Magus, in Acts 8:14-24, who tasted the heavenly gift, but whose heart remained a 'captive to sin'. He experienced personally the reality of the heavenly gift, one might say he tasted it as he saw the Spirit's powerful presence fall on others. He had believed and been baptised — he would have bought the gift of the Spirit's power, if he could. He longed for such power. But that is no sign of spiritual life or growth.

They had been partakers of the Holy Spirit. If we understand the heavenly gift as the Spirit, or even as the general blessings of the gospel, it seems likely and natural that here the writer is thinking specifically of the gifts of the Spirit. We live in an era when this phrase is of special interest. Is it possible that the experience of a spiritual gift is *not* after all a sign of grace? The New Testament is prepared to go further. Such gifts may be possessed in great measure, and their recipient not even be a Christian. Did not Jesus himself say: "*Many* will say to me on that day, 'Lord, Lord, did we not prophesy in your name, and in your name drive out demons and perform many miracles?' Then I will tell them plainly, 'I never knew you. Away from me, you evildoers!'" (Matt. 7:22, 23). Later in the Gospel record, the disciples whom he had sent out in pairs returned and said 'Lord, even the demons submit to us in your name'. Jesus' reply is highly significant: 'I have given you authority to trample on snakes and scorpions, and to overcome all the power of the enemy; nothing will harm you. However, do not rejoice that the spirits submit to you, but rejoice that your names are written in heaven' (Luke 10:17-20).

They must not fall into the fatal error of confusing gifts in their
ministry with saving grace in their lives.

They had tasted the goodness of the word of God. Again we
find that the teaching of Hebrews echoes the actual warnings
issued by Jesus. It is all too possible to be those who 'like seed
sown on rocky places, hear the word and at once receive it
with joy. But since they have no root, they last only a short
time. When trouble or persecution comes because of the word,
they quickly fall away' (Mark 4:16, 17). I was a close friend of a
fellow-student of whom this was an uncanny description. He
responded to the preaching of the message of the Bible just as
Jesus described. In the words of Hebrews, he was like 'land
that drinks in the rain often falling on it' (Heb. 6:7). His
profession of faith was the talking-point of many non-
Christian students. His life was radically transformed, and he
devoted himself to Christian things. I have never met anyone
whose experience could be so clearly defined in the
expressions of Hebrews 6. Others might 'profess conversion';
this young man had been enlightened, and freely confessed the
transformation in his thinking; he had tasted the heavenly gift
and participated in the powerful influence of the Spirit. He, of
all people, had tasted the goodness of God's Word. Today I
never hear from him, and the last time I did his life was
morally in ruins. Tasting the good word of God, in itself is no
guarantee of going on to maturity.

They had tasted the power of the coming age. The same
word for 'powers' is used in Hebrews 2:4 and translated
'miracles' (= works of power). But in this context the reference
is probably broader than that; perhaps broader too than
'spiritual gifts'. The 'coming age' in the Bible is the era to which
the Old Testament looked forward, the age which would be
ushered in by the coming of the Messiah. That age has now
come, in Christ. Those who belong to him, says Paul, are those
'on whom the fulfilment of the ages has come' (1 Cor. 10:11).
The judgment of God has appeared in Christ; the resurrection
— the ultimate sign that the new age has arrived — has its
firstfruits in him. Now that we are 'in Christ' all that came
through him has come *upon* us. The writer's point is that when
a person comes among the company of people on whom the
last age has already dawned, he cannot but taste the powers of

that new era. But tasting them, however deeply, and being translated into that age itself by saving faith may not be the same thing. How mistaken then to regard such an experience as being a mark of spiritual progress.

At this juncture it may be valuable to summarise what is being said. It is that these sections of 1 Corinthians and Hebrews have something vital to say to today's Christian bombarded as he is by what can only be judged to be a surfeit of quick assurances of spiritual experience. *Many spiritual experiences are possible which do not in and of themselves produce maturity*. Rather, it is *our response* to experience which will determine our progress in maturity.

When we turn back to Hebrews, we find exactly this emphasis. These signs are no guarantee of their perseverance, and therefore no guarantee that God will persevere with them. But in fact the writer sees another mark in their lives, which suggests to him that God will continue to persevere with them.

> Even though we speak like this, dear friends, we are confident of better things in your case — things that accompany salvation. God is not unjust; he will not forget your work and the love you have shown him as you have helped his people and continue to help them. We want each of you to show this same diligence to the very end, in order to make your hope sure. We do not want you to become lazy, but to imitate those who through faith and patience inherit what has been promised.
>
> (Heb. 6:9-12)

In essence what he says is that it is a stronger mark of true grace *that we serve*. We will take up the rest of this study therefore with a summary consideration of Christian service as a mark of increasing maturity.

> Now I rejoice in what was suffered for you, and I fill up in my flesh what is still lacking in regard to Christ's afflictions, for the sake of his body, which is the church. I have become its servant by the commission God gave me to present to you the word of God in its fullness — the mystery that has been kept hidden for ages and generations, but is now disclosed to the saints. To them God has chosen to make known among the Gentiles the glorious riches of this mystery, which is Christ in you, the hope of glory.

K

> We proclaim him, admonishing and teaching
> everyone with all wisdom, so that we may present
> everyone perfect in Christ. To this end I labour,
> struggling with all his energy, which so powerfully
> works in me.
> I want you to know how much I am struggling
> for you and for those at Laodicea, and for all who
> have not met me personally. My purpose is that
> they may be encouraged in heart and united in
> love, so that they may have the full riches of
> complete understanding, in order that they may
> know the mystery of God, namely, Christ, in
> whom are hidden all the treasures of wisdom and
> knowledge.
>
> (Col. 1:24-2:3)

Three emphases arise out of these verses: they describe the
nature of the summons to service, the goal of service and the
cost of service.

THE SUMMONS TO SERVICE

It is one of the very striking things about the life of the apostle
Paul, and significantly discernible also in the lives of the
prophets of the Old Testament, that their *call* to serve often
dominated the whole character of their ministry. The
circumstances in which they were awakened to hear the
summons of God have a fascinating way of determining the
direction of their lives and the whole character of their
ministry. Paul often speaks of himself as an apostle, 'by the
will of God' (1 Cor. 1:1; 2 Cor. 1:1; Eph. 1:1; Col. 1:1). Here he
does not quite say that, but it is impossible to read that he
'became' a servant of the church in Col. 1:25 without
recognising that he himself fills this expression out with that
significance.

Paul recognises that service is a gift of grace. It is something
that was given to him. In fact wherever Paul discusses the
particular forms of service exercised in the church, he does so
in the context of the idea of *gift*. This is seen clearly in Romans
12:3-13; 1 Corinthians 12-14 and perhaps supremely in
Ephesians 4:1-17, where the service of the leaders and
consequently the service of the whole body of Christ, in which
members mutually upbuild one another, is seen as a gift of the

ascended Christ to his church (vv. 7-11). We will return to this thought but it must here be emphasised that this teaching has profoundly moral implications. For it is evident that two prerequisites arise if we are to exercise this kind of spiritual ministry to others.

In Romans the prerequisite to service is consecration of one's whole being to Christ. Paul is at great pains to point out, especially in Romans chapters six and twelve that God calls for spiritual, intellectual and bodily consecration. We are to be pure in heart, clear in understanding, and holy in all our physical members, yielded as servants of righteousness unto holiness (6:13, 19; 12:1, 2). It is a sign of our own pride when we engage in service without realising that at the very gate to it Christ stands beckoning us to this total consecration.

But alongside this, in Ephesians 4:15 and 1 Corinthians 13 there lies the other emphasis of the New Testament, that true service involves self-denying love for the Church. The principle that guides the husband in his marriage is the one that guides the pastor with his flock, and every gifted disciple in the exercise of spiritual gifts. It is the principle of being willing to lay down one's life for the sheep (John 10:11, 15). Of course, without this we may have *gifts* for our own ministry; but we do not have grace for the *life* of the servant of God's people, and we are disqualified (1 Cor. 9:24-27). On the other hand, it is this that will mark whatever service we render with the authenticity of the grace of our Lord Jesus Christ. There is nothing more awesome in its spiritual perils than to receive gifts for service and to employ them in what is essentially a self-regarding, rather than a self-sacrificing way. That is why the words of Robert Murray M'Cheyne to his friend Dan Edwards are relevant not only to pastors, but to all who engage in Christian service:

> Remember you are God's sword, — his instrument,
> — I trust a chosen vessel unto him to bear his name.
> In great measure, according to the purity and
> perfections of the instrument, will be the success. It
> is not great talents God blesses so much as great
> likeness to Jesus. A holy minister is an awful
> weapon in the hand of God.
> *Memoir and Remains of R. M. M'Cheyne* p. 282

These moral prerequisites which we find in the three great passages on the exercise of the ministry of the body of Christ lead us a little further on. For the biblical stress that service is a special grace-gift supplies the key to recognising a call to service. In particular it suggests four elements in recognising that we are in fact called to exercise a ministry in this way. (a) If service is a gift, one of its identifying features will be *the possession of gifts* by the individual. If we are not *gifted*, it is altogether unlikely that we are *called*. An elder, for example, needs to be 'able to teach' (1 Tim. 3:2). If that is to be so he must be able also to understand. But if these marks are lacking, we can safely assume that whatever gifts we may have we are not gifted for *or called to* that work. John Owen put the matter precisely when he said that: 'Gifts make no man a minister; but all the world cannot make a minister of Christ without gifts.' The principle applies in every sphere of Christian service.

(b) The second element involved in the call to exercise spiritual gifts is that of *character*. In the New Testament while the possession of gifts is not itself a mark of grace, the proper exercise of them demands the presence of grace. For example in 1 Corinthians 14:26-33, one of the underlying assumptions seems to be that those who exercise the prophetic gift should also exercise the grace of self-control. Similarly the bishop must both be 'self-controlled' and 'disciplined' (Titus 1:8). All the passages in 1 Timothy and Titus which reflect on office and ministry in the churches also emphasise the great importance of character, and we have already seen the emphasis on this in general in relationship to every spiritual ministry.

(c) The third element is that of *desire*. That, it seems, is also part of the gift and the calling of God. We have sometimes simply accepted the apparently spiritual heritage of our forefathers at this point, and it is still often said that the one way to be sure God calls us to some form of service is if it is the last thing on earth we want to do. In many cases that sense of reluctance will be a natural response to the call of God. But in the cases of the biblical figures who show a measure of reluctance to respond to the divine call, it is not difficult to see that the real crux is not that they were unwilling to serve God, so much as the fact that they were fearful of what was involved. And that spirit often goes hand in hand with a very

deep desire to serve in Christ's name. This is what lies behind
the words of Paul in 1 Timothy 3:1: 'If anyone sets his heart on
being an overseer, he desires a noble task.' Aspiration and
desire were clearly legitimate in the apostolic church; and it is
one of the prominent features of the lives of many men of God
that they have similarly desired to do the very best they can in
Christian service.

(d) The fourth element is what we might call 'recognition'. In
Colossians 1:25, Paul emphasises that his office was given to
him *for others*. There is a similar thought in Ephesians 3:1,
where he says that he is a prisoner *for the Gentiles*. Now, there
are several things we might learn from this kind of attitude, but
one is this. If we are to exercise a ministry we may need the
encouragement that others benefit by it. This is the external
aspect of God's calling to ministry. Gifts, character, desire —
we may have a sense that God has graciously given us these.
But it is also his normal way of working to give us this external
assurance, perhaps through the encouragement of others, or
through evident seals that he is using our gifts. It is this notion
which ultimately culminates in the idea of ordination in some
churches.

Paul suggests that service is a tremendous responsibility.
Service means to live for others (Col. 1:24, 25; 2:1) and, more
particularly, is a commission. The word is *oikonomia*, and
means a stewardship. Paul uses many words to describe
service: it means becoming a *doulos*, or slave of Christ; it
means also *leitourgia*, spiritual ministry; *diakonia,* giving
support, making preparation for others; *hupēretēs*, becoming
an under-rower in the galley of Christ. But possibly this word
oikonomia gives us the most fruitful of all the word-pictures
for service. In the New Testament there are at least four ideas
associated with it. In Luke 12:42, the steward gives the family
its set portion; in 1 Corinthians 4:2, stewards are to be faithful.
In Titus 1:7, they must be blameless, or as A. T. Robertson
suggests, 'first-class'. There are no second-class passengers,
and no second-class stewards in the church. In 1 Peter 4:10,
they are to be hard-working.

The demands of Christian service are immense. Hard work!

'Having gifts that differ according to the grace given to us, *let us use them*' (Rom. 12:6 RSV).

Again there is this emphasis on faithfulness. Sometimes in our most depressed moments someone will put his arm upon our shoulder and say: 'Now, do not be despondent, it is not success Christ looks for, but faithfulness.' It may be that is a word we need to hear. But the sad truth for so many of us is that it is possible to be successful without being faithful; and faithfulness is a standard of a quite different, and higher order from that of success. John Owen once said that he knew of nobody who had ever been helped to Christ by his ministry. The records tell a different story, and we know of people converted under his preaching gifts. But his twenty-four volumes of detailed writing evidence the character of his faithfulness and make most of us feel that success would have been altogether a more leisurely pursuit.

It is not at all surprising therefore if the characteristic biblical response to the call to the ministry is one of strong desire *and* natural reluctance inextricably interwoven in the same soul.

THE GOAL OF SERVICE

In Colossians 1:25-28 and 2:2, 3, the task of our spiritual service is seen by Paul as being two-fold.

(a) **To honour the Lord Jesus Christ.** 'We proclaim him' (Col. 1:28). It is 'that they may know the mystery of God, namely, Christ' (Col. 2:2) that is at the forefront of his concern. That is necessarily the case. It is the work of the Spirit to magnify Christ (John 16:14), and all gifts for ministry flow from Christ through him to lead men back up to Christ. But how is Christ exalted, according to Paul's understanding? It is, he says, (Col. 1:25), when the word of God is made fully known. Of course he made it his ambition that this should be so geographically, as he says in Romans 15:19, 20, but he means this here in an *intensive*, rather than *extensive* sense. He means 'to give full scope to God's word'.

But again it needs to be emphasised that this is not only the task of the *preaching* ministry. It is the function of every gift. They are all, in some sense, ministries of the word, even if they do not all involve the preaching of the word. Whatever our gift may be it is of fundamental importance to the unity of the church, and the fulfilment of our own calling that we see the task of ministry being to make the word fully known, whether by teaching it, obeying it, or illustrating it in flesh and blood in our own lives, *in order that through it the Lord Jesus Christ may be exalted*. This was the all-embracing passion of Paul's life. We find him under threat of death in 2 Timothy 4:17 but what is his concern? He says, 'the Lord stood at my side and gave me strength so that through me the message might be fully proclaimed and all the Gentiles might hear it.' This is to be the all-consuming interest of the life of every gifted believer, that the same may be true through our personal service to the Lord.

(b) **To bring Christians to maturity.** We see this in Colossians 1:28; it reappears in a most interesting way in Colossians 4:12, in connection with Epaphras. We have already given a good deal of attention to this theme, but there is a particularly important facet of it which appears here in *Colossians* and in the twin epistle to the *Ephesians*. Paul speaks in Colossians 2:2 of the hearts of the Colossians being 'knit together' (RSV). In Ephesians 4:12-17, he speaks about the corporate growth of believers through their mutual ministry of love. We have already seen that there are in the New Testament marks of maturity which are essentially *individual*. But in the context of the exercise of gifts in the church the marks of maturity are essentially *mutual*. They involve fitting together, and not being swept aside by every wind of doctrine. Instead, maturity means caring for the development of the body of Christ, and seeing one's place and gifts *in that context*. The point is that true ministry exemplifies this and also produces it. To have any lesser aim would be to see Christian service in less than apostolic terms.

THE COST OF SERVICE

What has already been said shows that there is a price to be paid in all spiritual service. But Paul also gives it special emphasis in Colossians 1:24, 25. We have seen his teaching that service must be first of all a divine commission. It is to be a Christ-centred proclamation. But if the example of our Lord and the apostles teaches us anything it is surely this principle: *There are no gains without pains.* Paul again draws attention to two things:

(a) **The suffering involved.** He mentions his sufferings in Colossians 1:24: 'I rejoice in what was suffered for you, and I fill up in my flesh what is still lacking in regard to Christ's afflictions, for the sake of his body, which is the church.' Elsewhere, in 2 Corinthians 1:5, and Philippians 3:10, he explains that his sufferings have a special divine purpose. But here he seems to take this a step further when he says that he completes what is lacking in the afflictions of Christ. These are daring words, and it may not be possible to assert dogmatically what they signify. They mean this at least: Paul experienced the 'left-overs' of Christ's sufferings; the contradiction of sinners against Christ fell upon the apostle Paul. But he says even more. His sufferings were for the sake of Christ's body, the church. That was the cost of his ministry to them. He was at that time, he says in Ephesians 3:1, a prisoner *for their sakes.* And yet, he says more, he 'fills up' these sufferings. He uses a most interesting verb, which means that Paul fills up the sufferings of Christ, *instead of,* and *on behalf of* the church. That is surely a very remarkable view of what Christian service involves. Paul was not some kind of perverted masochist delighting in suffering for its own sake. But he presents this extraordinary illustration of the truth that those who exercise gifts must also be willing in their exercise to lay down their lives for the sheep. A very similar statement is made in 2 Corinthians 4:7-15. This principle is often seen at work in the church. There is no doubt that those who are called to the service of others also find themselves suffering on the church's behalf, and at times, in the church's place.

(b) **The exertion required.** Paul is speaking with tremendous power: 'To this end I labour, struggling with all his energy, which so powerfully works in me' (Col. 1:29). He uses the Greek roots from which we get our words energy, agony, and dynamite.

Little needs to be said about that. The emotion with which he writes surely speaks for itself. This is a work which is both painful, and strenuous. But we ought to notice the balance in what he says. Nothing gives such rewards and blessing as exercising gifts for ministry. In Colossians 2:5 Paul says that he rejoices to see their good order. When he speaks to the Thessalonians of what he has suffered he tells them that they are his hope, his joy, his crown of boasting before the Lord Jesus Christ. They are his glory and joy (1 Thess. 2:19-20). This, for all who are involved at whatever level of service, is but the fulfilment of our Lord's promise that no sacrifice is made for his sake in this life without receiving a hundredfold blessing in return, and in the world to come eternal life (Matt. 19:29).

I remember seeing a poster on the notice-board of a church which captured this perspective on Christian service. It read:

WORKSHOP — INSIDE
SHOWROOM — UPSTAIRS!

For Paul it was the knowledge of the glory that is to be revealed that made the cuts, and bruises, and sometimes the confusing mess of the workshop of service in the church entirely worth while. When we share that perspective, and see that our service costly as it is has an eternal goal, we will want as mature Christians to employ our gifts for Christ's glory.

11
Running patiently

When we discussed the question of divine guidance, we noticed that it is closely related to the endurance of the Christian. It is as we are strengthened for endurance that we will come to know the will of God. The same word endurance (*hupomonē*) is also used by Paul in connection with love in his famous words already quoted from 1 Corinthians 13; love 'always perseveres'. In both cases we have seen how all this is related to growing to Christian maturity. James spells out *explicitly* what is *implicit* in these passages, when he says (using the same word *hupomonē*) 'Perseverance must finish its work so that you may be mature and complete, not lacking anything' (Jas. 1:4). He is describing the progress of the life of faith. Faith under trial produces perseverance (cf. Rom. 5:3) while perseverance in turn produces maturity. It is the same truth which Peter emphasises, in the words from which the title of these studies has been taken: 'make every effort to add to your faith goodness; and to goodness, knowledge; and to knowledge, self-control and to self-control, perseverance' (*hupomonē* 2 Pet. 1:5, 6). The frequency of this emphasis leads us to conclude that *perseverance* is a basic feature of Christian living. Indeed, in a slightly different context, Jesus stated that it is *only* through perseverance that we experience salvation: 'he who stands firm to the end will be saved' (Matt. 10:22); 'No-one who puts his hand to the plough and looks back is fit for service in the kingdom of God' (Luke 9:62). Perseverance is as important as initiation; continuing is as important as beginning.

In view of this, it is not surprising to discover that the Letter to the Hebrews to which we have repeatedly turned, 'The Letter of Christian Maturity' as we have occasionally subtitled it, lays great stress on the importance of perseverance:

> Therefore, since we are surrounded by such a great cloud of witnesses, let us throw off everything that hinders and the sin that so easily entangles, and let us run with perseverance the race marked out for us. Let us fix our eyes on Jesus, the author and perfector of our faith, who for the joy set before him endured the cross, scorning its shame, and sat down at the right hand of the throne of God. Consider him who endured such opposition from sinful men, so that you will not grow weary and lose heart.
>
> (Heb. 12:1-3)

THE EXHORTATION TO PERSEVERE

The first readers of Hebrews had at one time lived lives which were characterised by *perseverance*. The writer reminded them of those days somewhat wistfully:

> Remember those earlier days after you had received the light, when you stood your ground in a great contest in the face of suffering. Sometime you were publicly exposed to insult and persecution; at other times you stood side by side with those who were so treated. You sympathised with those in prison and joyfully accepted the confiscation of your property, because you knew that you yourselves had better and lasting possessions.
>
> (Heb. 10:32-34)

But there were serious indications that something had happened to dull the edge of their devotion and determination. It is an awesome thought that Christians of such calibre as these could show grave signs of inconsistency. Elsewhere the letter hints at the nature of this failure to

persevere. It mentions their 'drifting' (2:1) like anchor-less
ships, instead of a determined fixing of their hearts to Christ;
the danger of 'falling short' when they should be pressing on to
the goal of their pilgrimage (4:1, 11); the temptation 'to become
lazy' (6:12) and failing to 'show this same diligence to the very
end' (6:11); the insane 'throwing away your confidence' (10:35)
which seems to have paralysed their spiritual advance. So his
words to the Hebrew readers in the following two chapters are
to be understood in the light of this: 'You need to persevere so
that when you have done the will of God, you will receive what
he has promised' (Heb. 10:36).

The connection between the tenth and eleventh chapters of
Hebrews is this: in contrast to their present life-style, the true
character of the readers is that they are men of faith (10:39).
The implication is: true men of faith persevere. There follows
in chapter eleven, as an exposition of this, a definition of faith, a
catalogue of the heroes of faith and a description of their
perseverance. The lives of these Old Testament believers
indicate with great clarity that faith and perseverance cannot
be separated. Over and over again faith is evidenced by
constancy and continuance in the ways of God. Thus Noah
persisted in building the ark, trusting in the bare promise of
God. Abraham pressed on 'looking forward to the city with
foundations, whose architect and builder is God' (11:10). Faith
always looks to, and heads towards the future (11:20-22).
'Moses persevered because he saw him who is invisible'
(11:27). It is against this background that we encounter the
exhortation: 'let us run with perseverance the race marked out
for us' (Heb. 12:1).

Clearly, then, what Paul writes to the Romans has a special
relevance here: 'For everything that was written in the past
was written to teach us, so that through endurance and the
encouragement of the Scriptures we might have hope' (Rom.
15:4).

This word hupomonē which the New Testament so often
uses for perseverance has a decidedly military background. It
is used in that context to mean 'to hold out' 'to resist hostile
forces'. It is the picture of the Christian soldier we are given in
Ephesians — taking his stand (Eph. 6:11), standing his ground
(6:13) and standing firm (6:13) when the enemy attacks him on

all sides. Perseverance means enduring hardship like a good soldier of Christ Jesus (2 Tim. 2:3).

But in Hebrews 12:1, the writer mixes his metaphors. The Christian perseveres by standing in battle, but he also perseveres like an athlete in a long-distance race — we must 'run with perseverance the race marked out for us'.

HINDRANCES TO PERSEVERANCE

The analogy of the Christian life as a *race* is extremely suggestive. In the opening words of Hebrews 12, attention is directed towards the question of preparation and training. The athlete has to *train*, he has to engage in rigorous discipline under the eye of his coach. He cannot hope to stay in the race, far less win it, if he is encumbered by heavy clothes or by heavy fat which pulls against his will and makes it impossible for him to press on. So the Christian discovers hindrances in his own life, within his own heart as he endeavours to make progress in the Christian life. His confession will be that:

> . . . hindrances strew all the way
> I aim at thee, but from thee stray.

One of the many refreshing features of the writer of Hebrews is his straightforward honesty about the Christian life. It comes out once more in this context, where he brings into the open a number of the hindrances which the Christian may encounter in his personal race. Three of them in particular deserve closer examination.

Indwelling sin
We are to 'throw off ... the sin that so easily entangles'. It is likely that sin in general is being described here. The words 'so easily entangles' have come into our language as 'besetting sin', and may even be translated 'much admired'. But it would be wrong to think that this describes only certain 'special' sins in our lives. All sin entangles, besets and destroys. That is its inherent nature. Therefore all sin, every sin, and sin in any shape or form must be put behind us.

The presence of entangling sin often produces two different effects. Either we confess and feel our absolute sense of hopelessness and defeat, or alternatively we justify ourselves — at least in the sight and hearing of others, on the grounds that we have already made considerable advance — of course we are not all the way, but then, the situation is not so serious as it might be. Scripture bids us step outside our own assessment of things when we thus speak, for those are the accents of deception. Sin cannot be reduced to manageable proportions. Our responsibility where sin is concerned is not to seek to reduce it to a level which our consciences find acceptable, but to slay it!

> If your right eye causes you to sin, gouge it out and throw it away. It is better for you to lose one part of your body than for your whole body to be thrown into hell. And if your right hand causes you to sin, cut it off and throw it away. It is better for you to lose one part of your body than for your whole body to go into hell.
>
> (Matt. 5:29-30)

The word which the apostle Paul uses is 'mortify — put to death' (Rom. 8:13; Col. 3:5). Paul also makes frequent use of the words 'lay aside' which appear in Hebrews 12:1, which literally mean to take or put off a garment. It is a persistent echo in his teaching (Rom. 13:12; Eph. 4:22, 25; Col. 3:8), and indicates a decisive act, a deliberate rejection by our wills of a way of life characterised by sin.

The first hindrance therefore to perseverance is sin within.

Sluggishness

> Consider him who endured such opposition from sinful men, so that you will not grow weary and lose heart. In your struggle against sin, you have not yet resisted to the point of shedding your blood.
>
> (Heb. 12:3, 4)

The writer of the Letter to the Hebrews continues his use of the metaphor of the soldier or athlete when he points out the second danger — like the Galatians they 'were running a good race' (Gal. 5:7), but now that they had gone some distance and discovered there were still many spiritual miles to travel, they were downhearted and discouraged.

It should be noted that there were solid objective reasons for this sluggishness and spirit of discouragement. They had known extremely difficult times in their Christian lives: in 'earlier days' the writer says,

> you stood your ground in a great contest in the face of suffering. Sometimes you were publicly exposed to insult and persecution; at other times you stood side by side with those who were so treated. You sympathised with those in prison and joyfully accepted the confiscation of your property,
>
> (Heb. 10:32b-34a)

The closing chapter of the letter speaks about some of the difficulties which they continued to encounter. That was partly why they had become sluggish — but it was no excuse for being so.

Everyone knows a little of this experience physically. Our television commentators often point out how the longer distance runners go through 'a bad patch' in which the only question in the runner's mind is: 'Why should I stick at it when I seem to be making so little headway?' That has a very obvious application in the Christian experience — as the Letter to the Hebrews makes painfully clear. This sluggishness of spirit and the tendency simply to give up was clearly present in the lives of these Christians. They were 'drifting away' (2:1), and tending 'to turn away from the living God' (3:12). The writer warns them 'let us be careful that none of you be found to have fallen short' (4:1), lest they 'fall ... by ... disobedience' (4:11). When his warnings are most sharply delivered, his exhortation is most passionately expressed: 'We want each of you to show this same diligence to the very end, in order to make your hope sure. We do not want you to become lazy, but to imitate those who through faith and patience inherit what has been promised' (6:11, 12). 'Do not throw away your confidence ... You need to persevere so that when you have done the will of God, you will receive what he has promised ... But we are not of those who shrink back and are destroyed, but of those who believe and are saved' (Heb. 10:36, 39).

In the light of these exhortations it would be a foolish Christian who thought that sustaining a life of true faith and zeal is represented in the New Testament as a matter of ease. The reverse is the case. No temptation is more frequently before us than that of easing up.

The author puts his finger on two forms of 'sluggishness'. (a) *Growing weary*. This expression is used in James 5:15 where it clearly carries the sense of being sick or ill, lacking strength to go on, having lost it through the exertions of undergoing many pressures.

There was a very old lady who lived near our family when I was a small boy. On the day she died, I remember my mother telling us that her last words were, 'The sparkle has gone out of the water'. At the age of four or five, as I remember, these seemed strange and mysterious words and I wondered what they could mean. Was she holding a glass of water? I thought. Surely there was some deeper significance? There was — she was weary to be away from a body which was drained of energy and in which her spirit felt no ease. The liveliness which had once characterised her, indeed the sharpness of mind — and tongue — which we had sensed even as children, was gone. That is exactly what can happen in the Christian life. We cease drawing on the resources of Christ, we go downstream from the Fountain of Life, and we discover stagnant pools whose water has no sparkle — and we grow weak and faint for lack of refreshment.

(b) We are also prone to *lose heart*. Usually because we see little or no return for our labours, when the way ahead offers little or no prospect of fruit, and when we cannot think of any way in which we can change the pattern of our service to produce the harvest for which we long. When the opposition we experience — in ourselves to the work of the Spirit, or in the world to our witness to Christ — seems as strong as it ever was, what are we to do? Perhaps as you have come to this chapter this is exactly where you are spiritually at this very moment. What can be done?

But to the honest admission that such difficulties exist, a third is added:

Chastisement

> And you have forgotten that word of
> encouragement that addresses you as sons:
> > 'My son, do not make light of
> > the Lord's discipline,
> > and do not lose heart when
> > he rebukes you,
> > because the Lord disciplines
> > those whom he loves,
> > and he punishes everyone he
> > accepts as a son.'
>
> Endure hardship as discipline; God is treating you
> as sons. For what son is not disciplined by his
> father? If you are not disciplined (and everyone
> undergoes discipline), then you are illegitimate
> children and not true sons. Moreover, we have all
> had human fathers who disciplined us and we
> respected them for it. How much more should we
> submit to the Father of our spirits and live! Our
> fathers disciplined us for a little while as they
> thought best; but God disciplines us for our good,
> that we may share in his holiness. No discipline
> seems pleasant at the time, but painful. Later on,
> however, it produces a harvest of righteousness
> and peace for those who have been trained by it.
> > (Heb. 12:5-11)

There was a time in the not too distant past when
undoubtedly the chief danger of the chastised Christian would
have been to lose heart. But in many ways the pendulum has
swung to the other extreme and our chief peril now is to 'make
light of the Lord's discipline'. The Bible bears witness to the
disastrous results of such a response to the rod of God. But the
heart of the problem when signs of such an attitude can be
seen, is that it reveals little sense that we care at all for God's
approval or disapproval of our lives. There is nothing worse
than failing to be awakened when God speaks to us through
the events and circumstances of our experience.

But why should we either despise the chastening of God, or
lose heart under it? Are these not the most natural response?
Indeed an eminently reasonable response? For he is God — and
we are creatures of clay; what other response could we make?

L

Our writer answers with a very simple, homely, yet tremendously powerful insight, drawn from Proverbs 3:11, 12: it is those God loves he disciplines: it is his sons he corrects! 'God is treating you as sons. For what son is not disciplined by his father?' (Heb. 12:7). We should not make light of God's discipline, nor should we lose heart. Nor is it enough when things go wrong and life becomes painful for us merely to bow down to God and acknowledge his sovereign will. How easily Satan can twist such a submission into a resentment of his sovereignty. No, we bow before the sovereignty of our Father, knowing that his will is for our good and blessing. We know that his banner over us is love (Song of Sol. 2:4). We know too that nothing can ever approach our lives unless it has first of all passed under the banner of his love. Nothing in our lives is outside that love; everything which is contrary to his loving purposes is barred at the door; everything which presses through, however painful it may seem, comes with the label of his care tied round it, and we may accept it meekly and with safety.

The context of this exhortation underlines for us one of the major reasons for our failure to respond spiritually to the various exigencies of our circumstances: 'you have forgotten that word of encouragement that addresses you ...' (Heb. 12:5). They had failed to allow the living word of God (notice the present tense — 'addresses you') to mould and shape their perspective on their situation. It was not at that time true for them that God's word was a light to their path and a lamp to their feet. What we saw in the first section of our studies of their loss of appetite and dullness of hearing had the most practical repercussions. Perhaps they said: 'it doesn't really make any difference to our lives that we lack a hunger for God's word.' The tragedy is that this is exactly the effect of a lack of hunger for God's word. Lives with no difference. Instead of being different, they were indifferent. They had forgotten God's word. What the writer is urging upon them then, is that they should have a spiritual perspective on their lives, that is a biblical perspective. The measure of the blessing and stability this brings to the Christian's life is seen in the maturity of character in the life of the child of God who bows submissively and lovingly under his Father's hand.

THE ENCOURAGEMENTS TO PERSEVERE

It would have been impossible for the Letter to the Hebrews to have left matters there. The readers were conscious themselves of their problems without someone else adding to their burdens and leaving them to devise some means of bearing them. Rather their correspondent wants to give them encouragement to persevere and to help them to press through their difficulties to stable, mature Christian lives. He therefore points them to three considerations which are foundational for persevering believers.

(i) The race they are to run is *marked out for them*. There is in fact so much encouragement in these verses that we are apt to overlook the encouragement which is given in the first verse.

The picture is that of the course for the long distance, cross-country race being marked out and prepared by the officials. The same is true for every runner in the race of faith: God has already marked out the direction our lives are to take. He has a plan. This is what Paul means when he says in Ephesians 2:10 that we are 'to do good works, which God prepared in advance for us to do'. More than that, he describes the blessings which lie ahead of the persevering Christian in words which should not be limited to our heavenly destiny:

> 'No eye has seen,
>   no ear has heard,
> no mind has conceived
>   what God has prepared for
>   those who love him' —
> but God has revealed it to us by his Spirit
>   (1 Cor. 2:9-10)

Our greatest fear of an enduring and persevering commitment to Christ is *the fear of the unknown*. Our greatest comfort and encouragement lies in knowing that it is not unknown to God. Indeed, it has been lovingly prepared by him, for our good and for his glory.

(ii) The race *has been run by others*. It is 'since we are surrounded by such a great cloud of witnesses' that we are to run the race of faith. It is a matter of logic, suggests the writer — *since* one thing is so (we are surrounded by witnesses) *therefore* another should be so — 'let us run'. But what is the nature of this logic? There are several levels to it. For one thing, we should emulate those we admire, we should be stirred by their example to press on in our own lives. But the principle encouragement here seems to be the thought that the Old Testament heroes of faith suffered and achieved so much and did so without ever seeing the full glory of the grace of God in the person of Jesus — 'These were all commended for their faith, yet none of them received what had been promised' (Heb. 11:39). They recognised that they had been caught up into something far greater than themselves or even their own personal salvation — and that proved to be an enormous encouragement to them to press on. Since they persevered — how much more ought we who live in the full blaze of the Sun of Righteousness?

It is important to notice the way the writer frames his sentences here. He says that his readers are surrounded by witnesses and this knowledge should encourage them, but he does not encourage them to concentrate on the heroes of faith. On the contrary, their eyes are to be fixed upon Christ, for he is the greatest encouragement to perseverance.

(iii) The race *has been run by Christ.* We are therefore to fix our eyes on him who is the author and finisher of faith, who had the course leading to his joy marked out before him, who endured the cross, with its shame, along with the opposition of sinners against him, and now sits in triumph at the right hand of God. By doing this we will neither grow weary nor lose heart.

The significance of this exhortation is clear. When we concentrate our attention on the problems we face instead of on the Saviour we have we inevitably lose a proper perspective on our experience. So we are to 'fix our eyes on Jesus' (v.2). But more than that we are to '*Consider* him who endured'. The significance of this expression is liable to escape us in the English translations. But even in English 'consider' can have both weak and strong connotations — 'to look at' *or* 'to make one's calculations on this basis'. It is this second sense which is intended here. We are to look at our own lives in the light of Christ's experience, and particularly his death.

Christ's death shows indwelling sin in its true light. 'In your struggle against sin, you have not yet resisted to the point of shedding your blood' (v. 4). We have a long way to go yet before we have experienced the full struggle of grace against sin, as Christ did. But furthermore, the death of Jesus reveals our indwelling sin in all its foulness and darkness. When we drag our soul-entangling, long-admired indwelling corruption to Golgotha, and view it in the light of the cry which pierced the darkness of the afternoon on which Christ died — 'My God, why have you forsaken me', our sin is the *answer* to Christ's question. This is the explanation of the contradiction and shame which were poured out on Jesus — this alone interprets the abject loneliness, physical weakness, personal agony of the Cross — the sin which clings to me. When we truly *consider him*, we rid our minds of the notion that to abstain from outward acts of sin is the same thing as perseverance in the struggle against it. How can we live in that for which Christ died?

Christ's death shows sluggishness in its true light. The only way to 'not grow weary and lose heart' is by considering Christ. Of course we face difficulties which make us feel like throwing in the towel. But what are ours compared with his?

The prophet Isaiah spoke movingly of Christ's perseverance under trial:

> I have not drawn back.
> I offered my back to those who
> beat me,
> my cheeks to those who
> pulled out my beard;
> I did not hide my face
> from mocking and spitting.
> (Is. 50:5, 6)

This is how

> The Sovereign Lord has given
> me an instructed tongue,
> to know the word that
> sustains the weary.
> (Is. 50:4)

With such an example before us, joined to his loving concern
for us in all our trials — is it not a small thing that he should ask
us to endure to the end?

Christ's death shows our chastisement in its true light.
Chastisements, as we have already noticed, can be
discouragements, but ultimately only when they are seen in
the wrong light. The light in which we learn to understand
them, according to Hebrews 12, is the light of the Cross. Christ
endured it, not for its own sake only, but 'for the joy set before
him'. It was productive. In fact nothing should be clearer to a
Christian than the fruitfulness of the death of Jesus, in which
he was chastised by his Father (Is. 53:5, cf. vv. 10, 12; Acts 2:23;
Rom. 8:32). So it is with our chastisement, when we see that the
same Father is using the *same method* with us as he did with
his Son Jesus, we come to see that while,

> No discipline seems pleasant at the time, but
> painful. Later on, however, it produces a harvest of
> righteousness and peace for those who have been
> trained by it.
>
> (Heb. 12:11)

The two key words are 'produces' and 'later on'. In different
ways in various sections of our studies these ideas have
appeared, and here once more. God pursues his purposes
through all the experiences of the Christian because he wants
to 'produce' in us the image of his Son. That implies that when
we are presently chastised we ought to look forward to and
pray in faith that '*later on*' there will be reaped a harvest of
blessing from the work accomplished in our hearts in the days
of ploughing. We are constantly in the Christian race in the
position of the disciples in the upper room, to whom our Lord
said: 'You do not realise now what I am doing, but *later you
will understand*' (John 13:7). Only those who persevere can
understand that through every apparent obstacle to
perseverance God is in fact producing within his children the
very perseverance he seeks. Let your prayer in chastisement
be 'O Lord, produce in me a harvest of righteousness and
peace'.

Here then is the encouragement we need. 'Therefore, strengthen your feeble arms and weak knees! "Make level paths for your feet," so that the lame may not be disabled, but rather healed' (Heb. 12:12, 13).

'Let us run with perseverance the race marked out for us.'

12
Living maturely

We must now bring these studies in Christian maturity to a close. It will be recalled that the plan of the study has been three-fold; *firstly*, to stress the importance of maturity, and to delineate some of its major characteristics; *secondly*, to show how certain basic blessings of the Christian life enable us to 'find our feet' as it were, so that we can move on from a settled position as God's children; then, *thirdly*, we saw how some of the problems and hindrances to true spiritual growth are to be met. We have tried to accomplish this by means of some basic exposition of a selection of biblical passages.

The deepest needs we have as Christians are best met by the patient unfolding of the teaching of Scripture *in its own context*. That is why the format of these chapters, as expository studies, is not accidental. Such study produces a different quality of Christian mind and spirit from the mere 'proof-text' knowledge of the Bible with which we tend to be content. It certainly produces a quality of life which will not be found if we use the Bible merely as a sounding board for our own spiritual experience.

Perhaps an example here will indicate what is meant. I remember sitting in my study discussing with a young and intelligent Christian the many benefits of the study of God's word. He was at that time, he told me, studying Ephesians, and I was interested to hear his comments. I suggested to him that I had discovered that Christians tend to read the Bible in two

158

quite different ways. I put it something like this: 'If I had given you a notebook to write down the things you learned in studying Ephesians, at the end of the day would I discover you had written a month's diary of your own spiritual autobiography — how you felt, what you thought of your relationship to Christ, your own needs and failures; or, would I discover, perhaps alongside this, that you had written down a basic outline of what God says in Ephesians through Paul?' Perhaps you can guess his reply. He confessed to having very little knowledge of Ephesians and its message — after a month of daily study! He went home, and started his study of Ephesians all over again, and some time later told me that a minor revolution had taken place in his life and thinking. There were blessings in God's word which he had only now begun to discover. I believe that story could potentially be repeated in the lives of thousands of Christians today. That is why exposition of Scripture has been so basic to the pattern of our study of the principles of Christian growth.

How then are we to live a life of settled Christian maturity? How can we grow from being, in our own eyes, spiritual infants, to becoming people of developed Christian character? Once again there is a portion of Scripture which deals with precisely this question. It is one of the shortest of the Psalms, but as someone has wryly commented one that takes longest to learn:

A song of ascents

My heart is not proud, O LORD, my eyes are not
haughty;
I do not concern myself with great matters
or things too wonderful for me.
But I have stilled and quieted my soul;
like a weaned child with its mother,
like a weaned child is my soul within me.
O Israel, put your hope in the LORD
both now and for evermore.

(Ps. 131)

The first thing which strikes the reader of Psalm 131 is that it shares the same title as every psalm from 120 to 134. This is a feature which is not repeated elsewhere in the Psalter and it

demands comment. But it is not easy to give a definite
explanation of these words 'A song of ascents'. What is certain
is that the songs were sung at times of pilgrimage during the
latter part of the Old Testament era. Possibly at one time they
were gathered together in this way, just as in modern hymn
books there might be a section entitled 'Communion Hymns' or
'Hymns for Special Occasions'. But why there should be 15 of
them and why they should be called 'songs of ascents' is more
difficult to understand. Some scholars have suggested the
'ascent' is the pilgrimage to Jerusalem; or that these songs were
sung on the 15 steps leading from one court of the Temple to
another. It has even been suggested that the 'ascents' involved
are those of personal spiritual experience. Whether such a
pattern can be clearly discerned in these psalms or not, it is
obvious that they do move towards a certain goal and there is a
kind of spiritual progress in them, as we see the pilgrims
'adding to their faith' by the very experience of coming together
to worship the Lord.

Psalm 121 gives us the picture of the pilgrim contemplating
the dangers of his journey from some outlying village to the
great metropolis. He may not have made the journey before
and is concerned about the dangers and indeed the personal
cost involved. He is an illustration in his time of the young
person who weighs the cost of responding to the summons of
the gospel. But an older pilgrim gives him the encouragement
he needs and assures him of the all-sufficiency of God in his
care for him. So that when he arrives at Jerusalem he is able to
sing with great joy:

> I rejoiced with those who said to me,
> 'Let us go to the house of the Lord.'
> Our feet are standing
> in your gates, O Jerusalem.
>
> (Ps. 122:1, 2)

Later, as he views the city of Jerusalem, and his heart is lifted
up in praise to God, the psalmist muses on the life of the child
of God:

> Those who trust in the Lord
> are like Mount Zion,
> which cannot be shaken but
> endures for ever.
>
> (Ps. 125:1)

In Psalm 126, as he remembers what God did in restoring his people from captivity, he longs that God should show his power again:

> Restore our fortunes, O Lord,
> like streams in the Negev.
> Those who sow in tears
> will reap with songs of joy.
>   (Ps. 126:4, 5)

There can be little doubt that there is clear progress here in some of the practical lessons which he is learning about spiritual life. But there is more to come. He must enter into the fellowship of his people's sufferings, and learn the pattern of spiritual life which was to find its ultimate example in the Lord Jesus Christ:

> They have greatly oppressed
> me from my youth —
> let Israel say —
> they have greatly oppressed
> me from my youth,
> but they have not gained the
> victory over me.
> Ploughmen have ploughed my back
> and made their furrows long.
> But the Lord is righteous;
> he has cut me free from the
> cords of the wicked.
>   (Ps. 129:1-4)

It is perhaps not surprising that this is followed by what seems to be a deep spiritual trough:

> Out of the depths I cry to you,
> O Lord;
> O Lord, hear my voice.
> Let your ears be attentive
> to my cry for mercy.
>   (Ps. 130:1, 2)

Through this dark experience the pilgrim learned to *wait for the Lord*, and *hope in his word* (Ps. 130:5). Yet all this is but a prelude to what is essentially a personal testimony to David's experience of growing to maturity of spiritual life. He has two things to say: he describes the nature of the maturity he discovered; he also outlines the pathway he took to it.

A DESCRIPTION OF HIS DEVELOPMENT

In this short psalm what David is depicting is in the nature of a minor crisis in his life which took him from the stage of his spiritual infancy to the beginnings of maturity. He tells us that he has stilled and quieted his soul, like a weaned child with its mother. The picture is both vivid and homely. It is of the child who has been accustomed to a milk diet but has now come to the stage where the process must take place of being 'weaned' from milk and introduced to a diet of solids. That is not always a period of crisis, but it sometimes is; and it is a crisis of development through which it is imperative that the child of God must come. Some families bear the scars of the struggle between child and mother weeks after the weaning process has taken place. In natural, as in spiritual life, it is a time when great patience and wisdom are required.

David wants to picture for us in this way how he has come to grow in grace through the experience of spiritual weaning. Although he does not specify the nature of the crisis he had gone through, he does show us that one of the hallmarks of his emergence from it is his contentment with the provision which God has made for him. This balanced contentment is a true mark of maturity; it is a sign that we have come to entrust our lives to the care of our heavenly Father.

There are three things worth noting about it:

(a) **It is spiritual rather than natural.** Some people by nature are more contented than others. Some houses are the epitome of tidiness to such a degree that visitors may go from them feeling there was something 'unlived-in' about them. Some children's bedrooms are kept with exemplary neatness — others give the impression of the debris of a demolition job! Some ministers' studies are neatly arranged, while others show all the signs of a weekend burglary! We simply, by nature, background and example, have different levels of contentment, and different

levels of experience with which we can cope. In this sense
some Christians are more naturally mature than others. They
are more capable and at ease in company, perhaps less
inhibited in the use of their abilities than others.

But this is not the contentment and maturity which David is
describing. Indeed David was by nature contented and
adopted a remarkably mature attitude to life. But he had to
learn a new kind of contentment, not based upon his
upbringing or environment but based upon God and wholly
dependent on his provision. Perhaps that is why he hints at the
struggle which preceded it. So contented was he with his lot by
nature that he little enjoyed the rough process of character-
shaping which God used throughout his earlier life to make
him fit to be his king and servant.

It is this same lesson we have already discovered in a
number of different ways in our studies. The pathway to
maturity is not an easy one, nor always a pleasant one. One of
the things it does is to wean us away from what *naturally*
contents us to what will give us truly contented and satisfied
trust in God. True contentment, which goes with true maturity
has to be *learned* (Phil. 3:15; 4:11).

(b) **It is inward rather than outward.** Contentment with God's
ways which manifests itself in maturity is independent of
outward circumstances. Our natural instinct is to imagine we
would really grow in grace *if only* certain circumstances were
available to us. Were the place of our employment different; if
the housework took less time; if only a little more money were
available to leave us free from anxiety. Now it needs to be
underlined that Christian maturity is not dependent on these
circumstances any more than genuine spiritual contentment is.
How easy it would have been for Paul to have assumed that
only his release from prison, or only the relief of no longer
knowing the pressing pain of his thorn in the flesh could make
it possible for him to press on to maturity and to be contented
with his own situation. But in fact faith learns a very different
lesson: to be contented in the experience of abundance and loss,
sorrow or joy, publicity or privacy. Paul knew what it was to
be a weaned child of God, leaning with steady breathing upon
the love and care of God.

What is 'the secret of being content in any and every situation'? (Phil. 4:12) What is the difference between the child striving furiously during the weaning process, and the same child gently cuddling in to its mother? It is not lessons in dietetics! Rather it is a recognition of the *wisdom* of the provision which is made, and a bowing to the *will* which makes it. This is the great lesson every child of God needs to learn: that all things come to us from the hand of a Father who knows what we need before we ask him, and whose supply is as appropriate to us as the wisdom which has planned the best way for us. If we are to grow to maturity and experience true contentment we will need to learn what someone has called 'the lost art of stooping'. When, after all, did I last bow down before God and confess 'The Lord has done it, I will rest content in his provision'?

It is interesting to discover that Psalm 131 is written against a background of child-rearing which was very different from ours. We wean *infants*, but these Jews weaned *children* — sometimes when they were as old as four or five. It is one thing to wean an infant peacefully. It is really another thing altogether to wean a child whose character is already well on the way to formation, who has a consciousness of its own identity, and moreover, has a will of its own. At that age, gentle persuasion is sometimes insufficient, and a tug-of-war between the purposes of the parents that this hurdle should be crossed, and the child with all its self-will, must seem inevitable. That is often the case with Christians too, before they bow their wills to the will of God.

(c) **It is tested by loss.** This is the third element which underlies the picture which David's psalm sets before us. So long as a child receives the diet with which it is familiar, it rests content — at least at its own level of infancy. Moreover, the diet of milk is doing the baby good, and it satisfies. But it does not satisfy the mother. And in order for the baby to grow the mother must withdraw the milk. This is the moment of crisis.

Obviously we cannot make a direct, wholesale application of the picture to all Christians; that is not the point of the psalm. Not all babies have tantrums at this stage in their lives, or regard the solid diet as 'loss' compared with milk. But some do, and by the same token many Christians discover that it is in the loss of what is important or familiar to them that the real test of their experience lies. Many Christians in fact only come to a genuinely mature Christian faith by the loss of something which sustained them at a previous stage in their lives, but which really needs to be removed, or at least distanced from them if they are to press on with Christ. David's son Solomon expressed the same thought in different language by saying that it is better to have one handful with quietness than both the hands full with a vexatious spirit. Paul stresses his own experience in this area of life: 'I consider everything a loss compared to the surpassing greatness of knowing Christ Jesus my Lord, for whose sake I have lost all things. I consider them rubbish, that I may gain Christ ...' (Phil. 3:8). No wonder he urged the Philippians, 'Join with others in following my example' (Phil. 3:17); 'All of us who are mature should take such a view of things' (Phil. 3:15).

When we suffer loss, pain is inevitable. The loss of fellowship, when we move to another part of the country; the loss of employment in days of economic pressure; the loss of someone we love — how painful it is. But it is not beyond the power of the grace of God to use that sense of loss in order to bring us to a new contentment with his love, and a new stability and maturity in serving him.

HIS PATHWAY TO MATURITY

We saw earlier that understanding is not enough. We are still, for all our understanding, left with the question — How? What are the means I am able to employ to grow in the way Psalm 131 describes? The opening verse of the psalm reads like a personal testimony written by David which specifically answers this question. He tells us that he did two things:

(a) **He guarded the ambitions of his heart.** 'My heart is not proud, O Lord,' he says; he does not now resist the will of God in his self-sufficiency, nor assume that he knows the way he should take better than God does. The RSV expresses the sense well: 'My heart is not lifted up, my eyes are not raised too high.' He is not saying, in general terms, that ambitions are wrong. What he is saying is that our ambitions should be consistent with our calling, with the destiny which God has given us. There is nothing wrong in aiming *high*; there is something wrong when we aim *too high*. David's own life furnishes us with an excellent illustration here. There can be no doubt that David's ambition was to be king of Israel. Perhaps from the moment Samuel had anointed him with oil (or even beforehand, for who knows what intimations of his future greatness God had planted in his heart?) he had set his heart upon the throne (1 Sam. 16:12, 13). It can never be wrong to set your heart on the destiny to which God has called you. But it is always wrong to seek that destiny by the wrong paths, as David could have done so easily. We know of two occasions in his life when his ambition to be king, which was God-given, was put to the test by the opportunity to hasten the promised day.

In 1 Samuel 24, Saul pursued David in the Desert of En Gedi and searched for him in an area known as the Crags of the Wild Goats. Saul came into the very cave where David and his men lay hidden — to relieve himself, says Scripture, somewhat wryly. His men urged David on; now was his chance. After all, was he not destined to be king, and could this not be God's way of fulfilling his purposes? The temptation and opportunity were there, but David was held back. How could he lift his hand against the Lord's anointed? (1 Sam. 24:6).

Similarly in 1 Samuel 26 another opportunity arose when David and Abishai crept into Saul's tent under cover of darkness and found him lying asleep; 'Today God has given your enemy into your hands. Now let me pin him to the ground with one thrust of my spear,' said Abishai. David's reply breathes the same spirit as his earlier words:

> "Don't destroy him! Who can lay a hand on the Lord's anointed and be guiltless? As surely as the Lord lives," he said, "the Lord himself will strike him; either his time will come and he will die, or he will go into battle and perish. But the Lord forbid that I should lay a hand on the Lord's anointed."
> (1 Sam. 26:9-11)

What is the significance of this? It is that David's ambition to be king was held in place by a *greater ambition*, which was to yield his life in obedience to God, whatever the circumstances, and to seek his glory first and only. So he was prepared to wait God's time, because he did not harbour ambitions which were 'too high'. Such spiritual principles cost David a great deal. He suffered loss because of them. But he could not have been the man God intended by any other means. When in later life he allowed other ambitions to replace *this* ambition, he ceased to be the man he once was.

This is one of the great secrets of spiritual maturity. 'It has always been my ambition', said Robert Murray M'Cheyne, 'to have no plans as regards myself'; his ambition was to serve Christ. 'My ambition', says Paul in Philippians 3:10, 'is to know Christ.' That is true maturity — to know, whatever ambitions we hold, secretly or openly, that we can look at them without for a moment lessening or diminishing our fixed gaze upon our Lord Jesus Christ. The eyes which are tempted to drift away from Christ must be brought back to focus upon him supremely — or all is lost.

(b) **He controlled the preoccupations of his mind.** David, at least at this point in time, did not concern himself with great matters or things too wonderful for him.

At the end of the day there are few clearer marks of maturity than this. It is possible to tell a great deal about a man by noticing his preoccupations and the things which cause him anxiety. In this instance David could mean two slightly different things:

(i) *Things beyond his possession.* He was attracted, for example, by the throne, but so long as God had put it in the possession of another he refused to let his mind be *preoccupied* with it. Alas for David and the nation, his resolve weakened in later life. When so much was already in his grasp, he coveted another man's wife (See 2 Sam. 11-12). His life is a lengthy illustration of the fact that the contentment of the mature is secure only so long as his mind is disciplined within the boundaries which God has set.

But it is all too easy to illustrate this in the lives of men who have so much. That should not blind us to the fact that the same temptation faces those who have little. Jesus warns us that not only the *delight in riches,* but the *cares of this world,* can ultimately destroy the seed which has been sown in the heart. The same temptations are our common lot. If we are to continue to progress in grace, it is essential that we guard our preoccupations.

(ii) *Things beyond his understanding.* David means more than things he could not possess. In all likelihood, as we have seen, Psalm 131 reflects an earlier rather than a later period in his life, a period when, though chosen, anointed, and destined to be king, he was hunted like a criminal and forced to company with the outcasts of his society. He might understandably have questioned his calling and doubted the wisdom or love of God. He would certainly have found it intensely difficult, if not actually impossible, to *understand* God's ways with him. The words of Jesus to his disciples, which might have brought him comfort, had been neither spoken nor written: 'You do not realise now what I am doing, but later you will understand' (John 13:7). Nor did David know the words of Isaiah which were to bring solace to so many of God's people:

> Who among you fears the Lord
> and obeys the word of his servant?
> Let him who walks in the dark
> who has no light,
> trust in the name of the Lord
> and rely on his God.
>
> (Is. 50:10)

Nonetheless, David left what was beyond his understanding in the hands of the understanding of God. That was a real sign of the extent of his growth. Many Christians find, by way of contrast, that few things are more *inimical* to a steady growth in grace than a *preoccupation* with problems we cannot solve, difficulties which seem to exacerbate the trials of life, sorrows which can find no resolution in this world. Our hearts break and bleed when we see our fellow-believers undergo such enormous heartaches. But it is no mercy to allow ourselves or others to have dominion over our minds *in the way that only the Lord Christ should.*

The bringing of every thought into captivity to Christ in this
sense is all-important, and demands tremendous levels of
grace. But it is the only way. One of the most moving examples
of this is found in the story of Jacob, some time after his
experience of meeting with God at Peniel. Rachel, his wife,
went into labour as they travelled from Bethel to Bethlehem.
The birth proved to be very difficult — too difficult indeed, for
Rachel died. But as she lay dying, she said that the new baby —
a son — was to be called Ben-Oni; but Jacob named him
Benjamin. The significance of this ought not to elude us. The
prefix *ben* means 'son'; *oni* means 'my trouble or sorrow'; *jamin*
means 'my right hand'. It is not difficult to sense in the
poignancy of this situation one of the most powerful examples
of a man under immense pressure to allow his mind to be
preoccupied by a sorrow which was past his understanding.
Added to the shock and sorrow were his wife's dying syllables
— Ben-Oni — son of my sorrow. But with the most
extraordinary control over his mind, Jacob confessed that,
with the help of God, this child would be the 'son of my right
hand', a source of divine blessing! It is a supreme example of a
man who confesses: 'I do not concern myself with . . . things too
wonderful for me.'

So we are left with the impression that there is no easy way
to maturity; there are no short-cuts. That is why the psalmist
employs an expression in Hebrew in verse 2, which is the sign
of an oath — 'God knows if I have not stilled and quieted my
soul'. It is an indication of the seriousness and strenuousness of
the task. It had cost him a great deal. It is in the light of this that
David urges his readers to cast themselves once more upon
God:

> Put your hope in the Lord
> Both now and for evermore. .

Lay aside your own ambitions. Lay aside your own hopes. Lay
aside your own wisdom. Lay aside your own self-assurance.
Make God and his will your ambition. Make God your hope
and your only wisdom!

And shall I pray thee change thy will, my Father?
Until it be according unto mine?
But, no, Lord, no, that never shall be, rather
I pray thee blend my human will with thine.

I pray thee hush the hurrying, eager longing,
I pray thee soothe the pangs of keen desire:
See in my quiet places wishes thronging,
Forbid them, Lord, purge, though it be with fire.

And work in me to will and do thy pleasure,
Let all within me, peaceful, reconciled,
Tarry content my Wellbeloved's leisure,
At last, at last, even as a weaned child.

                                                                Amy Carmichael

Only in his grace and strength can we be sustained to respond
to the exhortation:

   LET US ... GO ON TO MATURITY.

For further reading

Growing up

John A. James *Christian Progress* (Baker Book House)
James Philip *Christian Maturity* (Inter-Varsity Press)
J. Oswald Sanders *On To Maturity* (Marshall, Morgan & Scott)

Standing firm

Oliver R. Barclay *Guidance* — some biblical principles (Inter-Varsity Press)
Elisabeth Elliot *A Slow and Certain Light* (Pickering & Inglis)
John Flavel *The Mystery of Providence* (Banner of Truth Trust)
James I. Packer *Knowing God* (Hodder & Stoughton)

Facing difficulties

Herbert Carson *Facing Suffering* (Evangelical Press)
Joni Eareckson *A Step Further* (Pickering & Inglis)
D. Martyn Lloyd-Jones *The Christian Soldier* (Banner of Truth Trust)
The Christian Warfare (Banner of Truth Trust)
Faith on Trial (Inter-Varsity Press)
John Owen *Temptation* in *Works* volume VI (Banner of Truth Trust)
James Philip *The Christian Armour and Warfare* (Victory Press)
Philip Yancey *Where is God when it Hurts* (Pickering & Inglis)

Pressing on

Jeremiah Burroughs *The Rare Jewel of Christian Contentment* (Banner of Truth Trust)
K. F. W. Prior *The Way of Holiness* (Inter-Varsity Press)
J. C. Ryle *Holiness* (James Clark)
John White *The Fight* (Inter-Varsity Press)